To Carol —
A mother with another
Andrew — a lovely name

EducAting AndrEw

A Promise Fulfilled

by
Virginia Lanier Biasotto

drawing by
Carolyn Blish

Virginia L. Biasotto
4-06

PublishAmerica
Baltimore

First printing

At the specific preference of the author, PublishAmerica allowed this work to remain exactly as the author intended, verbatim, without editorial input.

ISBN: 1-4241-0171-9
PUBLISHED BY PUBLISHAMERICA, LLLP
www.publishamerica.com
Baltimore

Printed in the United States of America

Dedication

In the spring of 2003, my ninety-year-old mother and I were sitting on her porch reminiscing about Andrew. Her questions awakened memories about the past, and I retold stories about how God had led us on that difficult journey to find the solution for his inability to read. In spite of some short-term memory issues, she hung onto every word. When I was finished, she said, "You must write these stories down."

I was flattered that she thought them interesting, but life's pressures didn't allow much time for writing. However, she was not to be dissuaded. I would get phone calls saying, "I know you are busy, but you must write those stories down."

One day it came to me that I had written them down. I wrote them down as they happened. I started to dig (I was never much at throwing things away). Low and behold, I discovered a large yellowed envelope with the word *Andrew* printed on it. Inside were a hundred or more typed pages. For a Christmas gift to my mother, I retyped them on the computer and presented them to her in book form. She is now ninety-two and reads the book about once a week. Guests in her home have to read it, too. She is very persuasive!

It was her encouragement that led me to submit *Educating Andrew* to Publish America, and it is to her that I dedicate it. If you benefit from reading Andrew's story, you have Alice Darby Lanier to thank.

Contents

Foreword

The book you are about to read is the story of a young man who could not read. This young man had very dedicated teachers who worked tirelessly to try to help him overcome this problem, but to no avail.

It is also a story about failure upon failure, personal as well as institutional, but ultimately it is a story of success.

I am familiar with all of this because I was that young man.

My story took place in the 70's, but here we are some thirty years later and there are literally millions of children reliving my classroom experiences, and for no good reason. These children have good minds. In fact, more often than not, their intelligence is well above average, but they struggle to read. Why? Is it because they weren't read to, or that they watch too much TV, or don't try hard enough? Those are some of the reasons given for illiteracy. For most, however, the real reason is that they haven't been taught *how* to read. There is no excuse for the system that has failed them. Fortunately, the approaches that were ultimately successful in teaching me to read are not only available today, but have been improved upon.

A personal message...

...to those mothers and fathers who are about to read this book. Your son or daughter *can* be taught to read. Even adults who have been passed through the system, sometimes with diplomas, can learn to read as I finally did.

...to the educators. There are ways to teach those who seem to be unteachable. Don't be satisfied until you learn what it takes to reach all of your students. You'll feel gratified knowing that you unlocked the written word for your hard-to-teach kids and kept them from experiencing the frustrations I had.

...and to those who are going through what I went through. It's not your fault. You *can* learn to read. And trust me. You may struggle to read and spell, but I guarantee that God has given you special gifts that people who read and spell easily don't have. When the going gets tough, just think, "I could be another Edison, Einstein, or Da Vinci!"

Andrew C. Biasotto

Andrew

"Andrew. Do you know that your shoes are on backwards, your socks don't match and your shirt is wrong side out and backwards?" Lawrence, my impeccably dressed husband, confronted our four-year-old son.

Andrew glanced down quickly and then casually responded, "D-d-d-dad. I've got more important things to think about."

Andrew's mind was never still. He wanted to know the answers to questions that puzzled him. What's above the sky? What's under the ground? How many nails did it take to build that building? What's on the other side of that swimming pool wall? When he started asking questions, we were trapped into doing some heavy

Andrew, age 5

9

thinking. He strained the brain. He also strained the patience because of his halting speech. It seemed as though his tongue got in the way. If any of this bothered him, however, it didn't show. He was a happy-go-lucky little boy who loved everybody in general and life in particular.

Kindergarten was one continuous wood shaving, as Andrew's sole interest was the wood shop. Day after day he proudly brought home plastic containers full of wood shavings. I tried not to let it worry me that, while Andrew played, the other children were learning their colors, letters and other academic subjects. I assumed that he would catch up when he entered first grade. After all, boys will be boys, and Andrew was a November baby, making him one of the youngest in his class.

Then, at the end of the year, his teacher recommended another year of kindergarten. Like other parents in this situation, we agonized over making the right decision. Eventually, we decided to let him go on to the first grade, where we hoped he would catch up with his peers.

Several months into the first grade, however, it became quite clear that he wasn't catching up. The open-space, ungraded school that he was attending provided plenty of freedom for diversion from unpleasant activities such as reading and writing. Andrew was a concern for his teacher, who couldn't understand why he wasn't reading. Since he was obviously bright, she could only assume that his reluctance to participate was due to laziness, so he was frequently kept in from recess because of his inattention.

The end of the school year brought unwanted news. It was recommended that Andrew repeat first grade. This time the decision wasn't as difficult to make, since my husband's company had just transferred us from Maryland to California. A fresh start in a new school seemed made to be in order.

On the last day of first grade, Andrew's teacher signaled me to wait. "I don't know why Andrew isn't learning," she said earnestly, "but I do know that he is one of the happiest children I have ever taught. Whatever you do, don't let him lose his love of life!"

I pondered her words as I drove home. *How*, I wondered, *can we ensure a happy school environment for a child whose needs are a mystery?*

Andrew enjoyed a relaxing summer, the last for many years. He idled away the days building forts behind our house and exploring in the woods with children in the neighborhood. In August, we moved to Los Angeles and enrolled our three children in the local public school. We thought it was best not to mention Andrew's previous difficulties when we first met his second first grade teacher, Mrs. Thompson. This would later prove to be a mistake. Our hope was that his problems in kindergarten and first grade were based on immaturity and that time would solve all.

The first opportunity to meet and talk to Mrs. Thompson came at the fall open house. We stood in line with other anxious parents to ask that all important question. "How is he doing?"

"Everything is fine," she assured us. "Your son is keeping up with the other children. He's quite a talker. Keeps me on my toes."

I could sense the kindness of this young teacher, and felt grateful that someone who was patient and caring was teaching Andrew. Her words were very reassuring, and we returned home confident that our worries were behind us. In a few weeks, however, things changed dramatically.

"When I put a book in his hands, he looks at the ceiling," Mrs. Thompson said to me right after she had introduced her class to reading. "It's a puzzle to me why he won't even try."

On the spot, I volunteered to help out with her poorest readers; however, I soon found that my teaching degree had not prepared me to instruct, only to inspire. At that time, education professors taught that children will learn to read when they are ready. They believed that some children need to be prodded with questions to stimulate their interest, but that those with sufficient intelligence will eventually read. Games were always good ways to stimulate the mind, so this was the avenue I took with my new charges.

One of my favorite games was showing a flashcard with a word on it to two children. The one who read it first was the winner. He got to move to the next child and another word would be presented. One afternoon, I flashed a card to Andrew and another child. The other boy read it first. Andrew's face turned scarlet and he yelled at me, "I wasn't ready! Couldn't you see I wasn't ready?" Frustration was written all over his face, and the words of his first grade teacher penetrated my mind like a knife. *Whatever you do, don't let him lose his love of life.* Tears welled in my eyes. I dismissed the other children and put my arms around Andrew. He was too miserable to respond. His body was rigid.

I went home that afternoon feeling very sad and discouraged. Instead of the happy joyful experience that school was for his older brother, Larry, it had become a chamber of horrors for Andrew. I felt that there was nothing I could do to change it. His pain was a wound deep within me.

Every day Andrew would bring home all of the work that he hadn't completed in school. For hours we would sit at the kitchen table and struggle through it. While other children played happily outside with friends, Andrew laboriously answered what should have been easy questions for him. My patience was tried to the breaking point, and often I would say in exasperation, "If you would just try, you could do it! You knew that word yesterday. You must know it. It's just a little word. I can't believe you don't know that. It's so easy. Just think!"

Andrew never answered back. He just fell off his chair dozens of times for a distraction and ever so slowly plodded through his work.

When report cards were issued in March, I opened Larry's first. It contained straight A's and superlative comments. Kara, Andrew's younger sister, was doing well in kindergarten. Taking a deep breath, I opened Andrew's report card. "No effort. No achievement. Kicking and spitting on the playground."

Don't let him lose his love of life, she had said. It appeared that it was gone, and Andrew was only seven.

Breakthrough

"Why did you request testing for Andrew?" the school psychologist inquired curtly over the phone. His tone indicated that he was not happy to have been given the assignment. "I can't find anything wrong with him. He's as smart as I am."

I sighed as I hung up the phone. Our hope for some kind of explanation vanished with his words. Perhaps he was wrong. Maybe Andrew really was not as bright as we had thought he was. Why else would he be having so much trouble learning to read? I had taught school for three years, and those children who had trouble learning to read were the children I mentally categorized as slow learners. What other explanation could there be?

The afternoon mail contained a letter from my mother. In addition to words of encouragement to me, she sent Andrew a gift of compound words that she had typed and then cut in half for him to put back together again. I smiled sadly at her efforts. He couldn't remember the word "the" for two days in a row. There was no possibility that he could read "today", "sunshine", "plaything", or any of the other compound words she had so kindly sent. I gave him the envelope anyway and told him that it was a present from Grammy.

He happily spread all the pieces of paper out on the kitchen counter and I returned to the sink to finish washing the lunch dishes. Two minutes later, Andrew issued a satisfied, "There." I turned around to see all of the words correctly matched. For an instant I allowed myself to entertain the hope that a miracle had happened in my kitchen. Staring at the words, my mouth formed the word, "How?"

"Easy," was his reply. "I just matched."

I studied the words carefully. The differences in the ways they were cut were very subtle, hardly discernable. In record time Andrew had seen the key to the puzzle and matched all of the pairs. I felt confused. *How*, I wondered, *can he be so quick to think and so slow to learn?*

The final conference with his teacher, Mrs. Thompson, was scheduled for April. Since we had kept in close contact throughout the year, I didn't expect her to have anything new to tell me. She was a very compassionate person and had sincerely tried her best to find a way to help Andrew. This afternoon her frustration seemed to match mine.

"I have tried everything I know and nothing seems to work," she said. "He has given up, and his opinion of himself is getting lower day by day. He is angry, and his anger is being expressed in playground fights. I feel as though I have failed him, but I don't know what else to try."

I fought back hot tears as I listened to her speak. Despair seemed to fill the room. The situation seemed hopeless. Mrs. Thompson had done all she knew to do. I had done all that I could do. The psychologist had found no reason for his problems in school, and yet Andrew continued to fail. Our beautiful, warm, loving little boy was being destroyed because he could not learn to read.

Looking at my watch, I was shocked to realize that the conference had lasted one and a half hours. It was time for me to leave. I stood and thanked Mrs. Thompson again for trying so hard. She had done her best and had given him a lot of loving attention. I didn't blame her for his failure to learn to read.

"You know," I said wistfully. "I really wish it were someone's fault. Then maybe there would be something I could do."

"I went to a lecture the other day," Mrs. Thompson began slowly. "It was about perceptually handicapped children. Some of the things the speaker said reminded me of Andrew." She opened her desk drawer and pulled out several sheets of paper. "Here," she said. "Why don't you take these to read." I thanked her and automatically jammed the papers into my purse.

Tears blurred my vision as I made my way out of the school. Several children who were happily playing on the swings called to me as I passed. I waved automatically, but said nothing as I walked hurriedly to my car. A suffocating cloud of despair surrounded me as I drove the short distance from the school to my home. There had always been hope, but now hope was gone.

Turning off the ignition, I leaned my head on the steering wheel. I wanted to be able to pray, but the words wouldn't come. Thoughts had ceased and in their place was a sad numbness. I felt physically and emotionally exhausted.

Larry and Kara were staying with my neighbor. *Nancy will send the children home when she sees my car*, I thought, as I got out and walked into the house. *No sense in calling her.*

Once inside, I made my way down the hall to our bedroom and shut the door. The empty house and the privacy of the room gave me permission to release my pain. I began to cry uncontrollably. Perhaps a better word would be wail. All of the anguish that had been held inside came pouring out. When it seemed that no more tears could possibly come, my mind turned to the future and the tears began all over again. I pounded the pillow and moaned. I knew the sounds I was making were those of a wounded animal and I felt a kinship with all mothers, human or otherwise, who have watched their offspring destroyed.

Gradually the tears lessened. I lay on the bed, emotionally spent. A knock brought me back to reality. Kara poked her head in the door. "I'm hungry. Aren't you going to fix dinner?" I looked at the clock and realized it was after six.

"I'll be right there," I answered, managing a weak smile.

Automatically, I washed my face, combed my hair and applied fresh makeup. I needed to look normal even though I felt anything but.

Somehow I went through the motions of getting a meal on the table. Lively chatter surrounded me, but I remained silent. After supper Lawrence sent the children outside to play. "What's bothering you?" he asked, sitting down at the kitchen table. I focused on the dishes in the sink, willing myself not to cry.

"I had a conference with Mrs. Thompson about Andrew," I began. "She doesn't know why Andrew hasn't learned to read. He couldn't even take the standardized test that she gave the rest of the class." I paused and took a breath fighting the lump in my throat. "Counting kindergarten, he has been in school for almost three years, and he still can't read." I vigorously scrubbed the frying pan, defying the tears that were once again threatening.

Lawrence stood up and walked over to the sink. "Maybe he isn't reading because he isn't smart enough," he said gently. "Maybe we have been fooling ourselves."

Tears made their way down my cheeks and dropped into the dishwater. "The psychologist said he is as smart as he is," I spoke haltingly. "He must be intelligent to ask the questions he does." My voice trailed off and there were no more words.

Lawrence put his arms around me. He didn't say anything but just held me while I soaked his shirt with my tears. It was comforting to feel his warmth and strength and to know that he shared my misery. I knew how hard it was for him to watch Andrew fail and to know that there was nothing he could do about it either. My husband moved mountains in his job every day. By sheer willpower and belief in himself, he made things happen, but with his own son he was helpless.

Bedtime arrived and I tucked in the children, heard their prayers and kissed them goodnight. Then I went into our bedroom and got down on my knees. "Dear, God," I prayed. "You gave me my beautiful second child, and now I'm giving him back. I know of nothing more that we can do to help him. From now on, he is Yours." I stayed on my knees for several more minutes in silence. There was nothing left to say. As I slowly got to my feet, I felt a sense of peace.

Walking into the living room, I suddenly remembered the papers Mrs. Thompson had handed me at the end of our conference. I took them from my purse and settled down on the couch to read. The title was "Perceptually Handicapped

Children. *"* I was not familiar with the word "perceptual" as used in education. I looked up "perception" in the dictionary but still didn't understand how it applied to Andrew's inability to learn to read. Then I scanned all of the traits of a visually perceptually handicapped child, and suddenly my senses became alert. Each one could have been used to describe Andrew. I read them several times. It was like a case history of my child:

late speech development
speech problems
difficulty dressing himself properly
difficulty with organizational skills
draws poorly
difficulty learning to read
cannot remember written words
substitutes similar sounding words ("busgetti" for spaghetti)
reverses letters when writing
good with spatial tasks such as puzzles
creative thinker

A sliver of hope crept into my mind. If Andrew was a perceptually handicapped child, then surely there must be a cure. I looked over the rest of the article, carefully searching for answers. There were none. I had just learned that Andrew might be perceptually handicapped, but I hadn't been told what to do about it.

Connie

The next morning I arrived late for a weekly neighborhood Bible study. Jackie, our leader, had just finished writing down prayer requests. She turned to me and asked, "Is there anything you would like for us to pray about?"

My mind was focused on Andrew, as I blurted out, "I think I may have a perceptually handicapped child. If he is perceptually handicapped, and I really don't know what that means, I need to know what to do about it." Most of the ladies were nodding empathetically, but the leader, Jackie, had a wide grin on her face. Her smile bothered me, and I turned to her and said, "Jackie, this is not funny. My child is going down the drain and I need help!"

Jackie's smile became broader as she leaned forward and patted my arm. "Believe me. I'm not laughing at you. I'm just happy to be able to tell you that your prayer has already been answered."

Before I had a chance to ask her what she meant, the front door opened and in bounced an attractive blond woman I had never met before. "Hi!" she said enthusiastically. "My name is Connie and I'm from Glendale. I've been trying to get here for about a year and this is the first morning that I was able to make it."

Jackie waved her to an empty seat. "Ginger thinks she has a perceptually handicapped child. Maybe that has something to do with your being here today."

"Well, praise the Lord," Connie beamed at me. "I've got two of them!" She proceeded to tell her story of frustration concerning her two sons, and how she had finally found help in a doctor's office. She had made an appointment for her sons with an ear doctor, thinking that maybe they weren't able to hear properly. The examination showed that both boys heard just fine. Connie told the doctor about all of their troubles in school. He listened attentively, and when she had finished he said, "I can't help you, but in the waiting room is someone who can." He then introduced her to a therapist from the Glendale Adventist Hospital who had just started a program for perceptually handicapped children. She had her sons evaluated, and when they were identified as being perceptually handicapped, she immediately enrolled them in the program.

My heart was racing, but I spoke cautiously. "Do you think Andrew could be tested too?"

"Sure he could. If you like, I'll call and make the appointment," Connie offered.

"That's great!" I said excitedly. "The sooner the better."

Connie called me later that day to tell me that Andrew would be evaluated the following Monday. I looked up Glendale on the map. It was 25 miles away by freeway. The California freeways scared me to death as a passenger. I couldn't fathom driving on them.

There is no way, I thought, *that I can drive Andrew to Glendale via the freeway. I will just have to find a back road route*. After pouring over the map, joining one street to the next, I finally derived an alternative to the freeway, but it would be at least a two-hour trip. *What in the world am I to do? Even if I can muster enough courage to drive over there, the evaluation will be over just when rush hour is at its peak.* Drivers in Los Angeles drove bumper to bumper at 70 miles an hour, and just thinking about it made me break out in a cold sweat.

Just then the phone rang. The voice on the other end belonged to Anne, another friend from the Bible study. "Ginger, I was very interested in what Connie told you about perceptual problems. My son has been having some trouble in school and I'd like to have him tested on Monday, too. Would it be okay if we went together?"

"Sure," I said, swallowing hard. Now it looked like I might kill four people instead of just two.

"If you don't mind," Anne interjected. "I'd like to drive."

I glanced at the map on the table and was flooded with relief. "Thanks, Anne," I said gratefully. "You can't know how much I would appreciate that."

Sure enough, the results of Andrew's testing revealed a visual perceptual problem. Anne was told that her son's difficulties were due to other causes. The therapist who tested the boys told me that the next program would begin in the summer. It was 1972 and treatment was based on Mary Ann Frostig's work. It involved coordination exercises, eye tracking and balance beam practice. Since I was so eager to begin, he arranged to give me some advanced instruction so that I could work with Andrew in the months prior to the course. This involved driving to Glendale. So with a death grip on the steering wheel and dripping palms, I navigated the freeways.

Putting into practice the exercises that they taught me was not as simple as I had expected. Larry and Kara wanted to be part of this new "fun," but Andrew would often walk out leaving his brother and sister on the floor doing prone jumping jacks or walking the homemade balance beam. He rebelled against the eye tracking exercises, too. His lack of cooperation created extreme stress because he was refusing the cure.

Decisions

It was during this time that I sent an audio tape of all that we had been experiencing to our good friends from Maryland, Joe and Pat Knepper. Before the week was out, they returned it with comments of their own. They found it interesting that Andrew's inability to read was due to a visual perceptual problem, and wondered if that might be the same thing that was interfering with their daughter's progress in school. Joe talked to a school administrator to find out if she could be tested and had learned that there was no training available in Maryland. The person he spoke to told him that there was a program at Ohio State University, if he wanted to take her there.

That week Lawrence was promoted. We were moving to Columbus, Ohio! "You think you were transferred," I teased triumphantly. "I've got news for you. Andrew is the one who is being moved to Ohio!"

Lawrence started his new job immediately, and I called Dr. Miller, who was in charge of the program for perceptually handicapped children at Ohio State. He listened as I described Andrew to him, and agreed that he would be an ideal candidate for the program. I learned that Dr. Miller's program wasn't using Mary Anne Frostig's perceptual training, but instead was based on something called "behavior modification." He seemed confident that this would help Andrew focus and learn. I signed him up immediately.

The class started on June 25th, only six weeks away, but I was not concerned since I felt that God was leading us in this direction. When people asked me what our plans were, I would tell them, "All I know is that we will be in Columbus, Ohio on the 25th of June."

"Have you sold your house yet?" they would ask.

"No, not yet."

"Have you bought a home in Ohio?" was usually the next question.

"No, not yet."

"Uh... have you arranged for a mover?"

"No. All I know for sure is that we will be in Columbus on the 25th of June."

Because he was busy with his new job, Lawrence wasn't able to have me come out to house hunt until the first week in June. I was sure we would find something that was perfect for us—size, cost, neighborhood—but we didn't. After a week of looking, we knew the area we wanted to live in, but all of the houses were out of our financial reach. I returned to Los Angeles without the security of knowing that we had a home to move into. Amazingly, my confidence wasn't dimmed. Somehow we would be in Ohio on the 25th of June.

Our neighbors probably thought I was a bit demented, but they went along with my assertion that as of June 25th, we would be living in Columbus, Ohio. A farewell party was planned for June 16th. Again, many people inquired about our plans. If

Lawrence was asked, he would usually gesture in my direction and I would tell them, "No, our house is not sold. No, we haven't purchased another house in Ohio. But we will be in Columbus in time for Andrew to begin summer school at Ohio State University on the 25th of June."

In the course of one such conversation, I learned that movers were on strike in Los Angeles. When asked, I admitted that we had not contacted a moving company yet. "Good luck," my friend said, and the look on her face said that she thought we were really going to need it.

On Monday, June 18th, Lawrence called me from Columbus. "I've made an offer on a house, but they turned me down. I don't feel that I can go any higher."

"Fine," I replied cheerfully. "Something else will come along."

The next day he called again. "I've made an offer on another house, but they turned me down, too."

"Don't worry," I consoled him.

On Wednesday he called again. "This is ridiculous. I am not going to buy something we can't afford just because you think that Andrew has to be in that school on Monday. This is the height of the fire season in the San Fernando Valley. For us to leave our house and all our possessions would be crazy. Be reasonable. This idea of yours just isn't working out!"

Up until now, he had been supportive of my desire to get to Columbus by the 25th of June. His frustrations were understandable, but my zeal to protect my child overrode everything else. "I don't care about our possessions. What I do care about is getting help for Andrew. We can come and live in your motel room."

"That's impossible," he retorted. "The company would never go for that!"

"Then we'll live in a tent!" I shouted into the phone. "All I know is that Andrew has to be in that school on Monday morning." With that last outburst, I hung up the phone. Immediately, I was overcome with remorse. My mind accused me. *He was just trying to be practical. He wants help for Andrew as much as I do. What kind of witch am I? Maybe all of this is just my idea. Maybe it is my imagination that makes me think that God is orchestrating our move to Ohio. Surely things would be going smoothly if it was part of God's plan.* I felt miserable, and for the first time, unsure.

I was seriously considering calling him back when the phone rang. A very unsmiling voice said, "I have called the company representative and told him I have to be moved to Columbus by this weekend. He told me that would be impossible because the movers they normally use are all on strike. I told him to do his best because my marriage might be at stake. He asked me for an address in Ohio. I told him to tell the movers to call me when they were an hour from Columbus and I would tell them where to take the furniture. If they can get a mover, they will call you. There's nothing more that I can do."

I felt sick. What had I done? We had no place to go. No where to put our furniture. We hadn't sold our house so we didn't know how much money we could spend for a new one. I could hardly breathe as I mumbled a tearful apology to my husband.

After hanging up, I sat motionless for several minutes. The enormity of the situation was overwhelming, but the die had been cast. If a mover could be contacted, we would be in Columbus on the 25th of June and that, after all, was what I wanted.

An hour later, the phone rang again. This time it was the company representative calling for me. "Mrs. Biasotto, you will be contacted about the weight of your household goods shortly. We got a moving company to drop a load they were picking up in San Francisco and come back to Los Angeles to move you. Their packers will arrive tomorrow morning and move you on Friday. If there is anything I can do, feel free to call." His words were cordial, but his tone of voice indicated strained annoyance.

I managed a feeble, "Thank you," and hung up the phone. Suddenly, all of the things I had to do began to register in my mind. *Cancel mail delivery. Pick up medical records at the pediatrician's office. Get Lawrence's car at the airport. Order extra insurance on our house in case of fire.* The list went on.

The rest of the afternoon was a blur of activity. The fact that Los Angeles was in the middle of a record-breaking heat wave didn't help matters. The next day was predicted to be 114 in the shade and our air conditioner stopped working. After dinner, a neighbor came over to take a look at it and pronounced it "dead." Because of the demand, he didn't think I would be able to get a repairman for several days.

That night I lay awake worrying. *The heat in the house will be unbearable. The packers will surely pass out without air conditioning.* My mind presented question after question, but no answers, as I tossed and turned. About three in the morning, I had another conversation with God. "If this is Your plan for us to move to Ohio, please make the air conditioner work for the packers." I finally fell asleep. When I awoke, the house was cool. The air conditioner ran until 5 pm the next day and then died forever.

Friday at noon, Lawrence called. "I have bought you a house. We can move in immediately." His words were spoken with enthusiasm, so I knew that he was no longer upset with me for causing all this trouble. It was the first house he had bid on. The owners had reduced the price and we could now afford it.

Saturday, I was busily scrubbing the floors of our empty house when a realtor called to see if he could bring someone by to look. "Of course," I replied. "I'll be here for several hours."

They arrived and made a quick tour. Andrew volunteered that the air conditioner was broken, as he assisted the realtor in showing the house. The couple said a polite, "Thank you," before leaving. I never expected to see them again.

At 3:45, fifteen minutes before I was to lock the doors and left forever, the realtor called to tell me that the couple had bought our house at our price, even though it had been appraised for less. They wanted to move in immediately!

I found a piece of paper in my purse and wrote down the pertinent information. In a joyful daze, I called Lawrence. "Our house is sold!"

Ohio was waiting and Andrew was going to be in school on Monday!

Explanations

Andrew, age 8

The program, sponsored by Ohio State University, was based on B. F. Skinner's theory of behavior modification. In addition to math and reading instruction, students were bribed with redeemable coupons to keep their feet on the floor, raise their hands, turn in their homework, etc... It seemed like a roundabout way to correct a perceptual problem, but who was I to question the methods of a great university? The trip from our home to the school in downtown Columbus was twenty-two miles. Since Larry and Kara were too young to be left alone and too active to wait with me, I drove two round trips a day with them in order for Andrew to be able to learn to read. I fully expected that after summer school, he would be ready to join his peers in a normal second grade experience.

The school psychiatrist who faced me across her desk was young and enthusiastic. She had just received her Ph.D. in a field called Learning Disabilities. "Andrew," she declared, "is learning disabled."

"Whatever happened to his perceptual problem?" I asked innocently.

"That's part of his learning disability," she assured me patiently. "Try to think of it this way. Information is going into the brain and for reasons we don't understand, there is a short circuit and the child is not able to readily recall and use this information."

"That sounds very serious," I said to her. "What can be done to help a learning disabled child learn to read?"

She ignored my question and went on with her explanation. "Most children are able to read by storing pictures of words in their brains. When I say 'cat,' do you see the word cat in your mind?"

"Yes, I do," I said, mentally picturing the three letters on an imaginary screen.

"Learning disabled children who have a visual perceptual problem don't see the word. If they have a strong auditory sense they learn the sounds of the letters and read by blending the sounds together. Andrew will have a reading teacher who will teach him to do this." She spoke with authority.

I thanked the young psychologist and once again felt hopeful that this new direction would prove to be the *cure* we had been looking for. On the way home I reviewed in my mind all that I had heard so that when Lawrence came home that evening, I would be able to remember at least half of it to share with him. *Andrew will have a teacher who will teach him the sounds of the letters, so that he can blend them together and read.* It made sense.

School began and true to her word, the psychologist arranged for Andrew to have special reading tutoring three times a week. Because of the great demand on her time, Mrs. Greenstreet could only give him fifteen minutes per session, which was shared with another child.

Progress was slow, very slow. Andrew spent much of his time walking around and investigating the classroom. Not being familiar with behavior modification, his teacher tried to curb his restlessness by providing him with a closed-in desk that was screened off from the rest of the class. This method of eliminating visual stimuli might have worked if the assignments he was being asked to complete were within his grasp. As it was, he could not read the instructions to workbook pages, nor could he read any printed matter. Although he understood the math concepts, his writing was so poor that the numbers were illegible. Many were reversed. It seemed as if his abilities ended when a pencil was put in his hand.

In spite of the frustrations of his school routine, Andrew seemed optimistic and happy. He never balked at going to school, and his teachers tried their best to help him fit in. His high level of activity and his short attention span could be improved by medication, we were told. The pediatrician prescribed Ritalin.

He did sit a bit longer in his chair, but at night he stared at the ceiling unable to fall asleep. Often I would catch him swaying dizzily at the top of the stairs before grabbing hold of the railing and carefully walking down. All of this disturbed me greatly, but the teachers at school insisted that it was helping and the doctor said that in time his body would get used to the drug. Somehow it seemed wrong.

Mercifully, second grade ended and Andrew's teacher proudly announced that he had achieved a full year's growth in reading, which put him just past the primer level into the first grade. We were glad for the progress, but he would still be two years behind his class when he entered the third grade. Socially, the lag was taking its toll. He knew that he was behind the other children. Although he didn't voice his fears, it was obvious that the other students thought he was stupid. Subconsciously, he was beginning to agree with them.

Andrew's desire to make friends was so great that he smothered anyone who seemed receptive to his friendship. Often he gave away favorite possessions in the hope of winning the friendship of a classmate. Clowning for attention gained him laughs, but those who laughed rarely stayed to play. If the Ritalin had to be administered while another child was in our home, I would try to do it secretively, but Andrew would invariably wave it under the child's nose announcing that he took pills to make him smart. I felt like I died a little each time one of these situations occurred. Later I would try to explain to Andrew that what he was doing was actually driving children away instead of encouraging them to be his friends. His response was fury at me expressed by an angry glare as he yelled, "Leave me alone!" Later he added a painful squeeze to my arm, or some other physical manifestation of his displeasure. I didn't realize until much later that my attempt to help had compounded the problem. He was struggling for the acceptance of not only his peers, but also of his mother.

Family

It was garage clean-up time. The whole family was busily involved in removing bicycles, toys, garden supplies, old tires and a multitude of other household necessities from the garage so that the annual hose down could occur. Lawrence was unusually quiet. He responded negatively to my inquiry as to what was bothering him. Knowing that prodding would do no good, I chatted with the children and left him alone.

"What would you think about another move?" His words came as a bombshell. We had been in our Ohio home for just nine months. The last drapes had just been hung, the children and I had made friends in the community, and I was looking forward to settling in for a long stay. We all stopped what we were doing and stared at him. Larry was the first to break the silence. "I don't want to go. I like it here."

Kara was less diplomatic. "I'm not leaving!" she stated with finality.

"It's okay with me, Dad," Andrew told him. "It might be interesting."

How ironic, I thought. *The child who needs stability the most is the most receptive to change.*

"The company is closing the Columbus office and they want to send me to Portland, Oregon."

"Portland, Oregon!" we all echoed as one. Living in California so far from our Delaware family had been a lonely experience. Now we were being told that we would have to again be separated by the width of the continent. The children missed the joys of close contact with their grandparents. Ohio was a day's drive, but Oregon would mean a yearly flight at most.

My heart sank. I thought about Andrew. Another move would mean retesting and a search for a school that would meet his needs. A second disadvantage concerned Lawrence's parents. His dad was being treated for Hodgkin's disease, and we wanted to be as close to him and Mom as possible. It just didn't seem right that we should go so far away at this particular time. The rest of the garage cleanup was subdued. Each of us in his own way was trying to adjust to another uprooting.

That night I had another conversation with God. "If this is Your plan, Lord, I know it is for the best. But if it is possible not to go so far away from the East Coast, we would like it much better."

Monday morning the phone rang and my husband's excited voice said, "You won't believe this! My transfer to Oregon has been changed. We're going to Philadelphia!"

From toddler...

... to teen

Glasses

On June 21, 1974, exactly one year since we moved into our Columbus home, we moved out. This time we were heading for an apartment while we waited for our new home to be built in Wilmington, Delaware, a short commute to Philadelphia and close to our parents. By this time, my father in law's cancer had progressed and he was very sick.

Andrew and Kara

The school Andrew and Kara would be attending was quite close. We investigated several before deciding where to put down roots. We selected Lombardy Elementary School because of the excellent reputation of the Learning Disability teacher, Dorothy Stottlemeyer. She spent quite a lot of time with Andrew before school started. One of the tests she administered revealed an I.Q. of 133. Never again could his struggle with reading be blamed on low intelligence. Because of her recommendation, Andrew was assigned a reading tutor every day for thirty minutes. We were delighted. Finally, he would be getting the help he so desperately needed.

"There ought to be glasses to help children like me," Andrew said as we were driving from our apartment to school one fall morning.

"Glasses won't help a perceptual problem. You have perfect vision. Remember? We had your eyes checked in California," I replied.

"I know," Andrew answered absently. "But when I grow up I'm going to invent glasses to help kids like me."

I remained silent, wishing that something as simple as glasses could provide the solution to his disabilities.

After dropping the children off at school, I drove over to my new neighborhood to have coffee with Betty, a new friend. We talked about our husbands' work, where we had lived and, of course, our children.

"Our oldest son is in college and doing well," Betty began, "but things were pretty rough for him before he got his glasses. School was a struggle until he was sixteen."

"You mean you didn't have his eyes checked until then?" I asked incredulously.

"Oh, no," she responded. "He had many exams, but it wasn't until an optometrist specializing in children with learning problems examined him that we discovered the difficulty."

My senses became acutely alert as I hung onto her every word. "What did the doctor find out?"

"He discovered that each eye was seeing correctly, but when used together they were not focusing properly. When he would begin to read a line of print, the second half of the line would become superimposed on the first. Can you imagine! All those years of frustration could have been eliminated by a pair of developmental lenses."

"Betty," I said, looking directly into her eyes. "My son has a great deal of difficulty reading. Do you think that maybe this could help him, too?"

"It might. What do you have to lose?"

Betty gave me the doctor's name and number. An appointment was made for later that week. After two hours, the doctor explained what he had found. "Andrew is using 60% more effort to focus than most children. He will sometimes focus before the word, causing reversals. 'Was' becomes 'saw' and 'dog' becomes 'god'. He should wear these developmental lenses when he is in school. You should see a great improvement in his school work." The doctor recommended non-breakable frames for obvious reasons, but we felt that Andrew would feel better about wearing glasses if he could choose the frames. We were told that the gold wire frames could be insured, so we signed up for complete coverage. There is no doubt in my mind that the Optical Store lost money on us.

"Can you tell if the glasses are helping Andrew?" I asked Mrs. Stottlemeyer.

"I can't see any improvement in his work, but he does keep them on, so maybe they are helping," she replied hopefully.

I had my doubts. Surely if they were going to make a difference we would have seen some by now. It was almost Christmas.

Mrs. Stottlemeyer was devoted to Andrew, as she was to all of her students. When most teachers were at home having dinner, Dorothy Stottlemeyer was still at school preparing lessons for tomorrow's classes. I had rarely seen such dedication in a teacher and we felt grateful that Andrew was in her Special Education class.

I stood up to leave, but Mrs. Stottlemeyer had something else on her mind. "I know," she began, "that Andrew's teachers in Ohio supported the use of Ritalin, but I really don't like it, and I don't think that it is doing any good. Would you mind if we stopped it and didn't tell the rest of his teachers? Then if they notice a big change in his behavior, we will know that it is real and not just what they expected to happen. We can ask them for an evaluation at the end of the marking period in mid-January."

"There is nothing I would rather do than stop giving drugs to my child," I agreed. "Because so many authorities told me it would help him in school, I believed them, but if you think we should stop, then we will. If you see a problem in school, let me know and I'll see how things go at home."

A month later third grade report cards came out. Two teachers commented about improved concentration in class. No one thought that he was overly active. As far as his teachers knew, he was still taking the Ritalin.

Help?

In spite of daily tutoring, Andrew made very little progress during third grade. He was still reading on a first year level. We hired a teacher to tutor him during the summer, but although he enjoyed her time and attention, no discernible progress was made.

As I paid for my purchases at the health food store, my eye caught the words on a poster beside the register. "Does your child have difficulty in school? Does he have trouble sitting still for long periods of time? Perhaps he has an allergy to artificial dyes found in many processed foods." The poster referred to a book written by Dr. Ben Feingold entitled *Why Your Child is Hyperactive*. Before leaving the store, I plunked down $8.95 and went out with the book under my arm.

Settling myself in a comfortable chair, I ignored the laundry and began to read. Dr. Feingold had proven dramatically that artificial ingredients, especially coloring in food and drink, can cause hyperactivity and in some cases, learning problems. Like most people, I shopped according to taste rather than ingredients, but after reading Dr. Feingold's book, I committed myself to purifying my family's diet. If Andrew could be helped by the Feingold Diet, then probably all of us would benefit. No longer did I breeze in and out of the grocery store.

Now, every label had to be scrutinized for suspicious elements. At first, the time spent shopping seemed endless, but after a while, I began to learn which mayonnaise to buy, which cereals were OK, which juices contained that terrible red dye…My family complained. Favorite foods were suddenly missing from the pantry shelf. Others replaced them that didn't meet their taste standards. Andrew often took the blame from his brother and sister because, "We have to eat this yucky stuff because of you!"

He stoically stuck to the diet, even in school when special birthdays provided *illegal* cupcakes and ice cream. Not only did his disability seem to make him different, but now he was also singled out because he couldn't eat what everybody else ate.

It was as difficult to evaluate improvement due to the diet, as it was to judge the value of the glasses. He still remained three years below grade level in his reading, and even though the reading specialist worked with him every day, he did not progress.

The end of the school year was approaching and we knew that summer had to be a time of work for Andrew. He might lose what little he had gained if allowed to play his way through the next three months. We decided that Andrew would live in Newark, Delaware with my parents, Charles and Alice Lanier, and attend the Reading Clinic at the University of Delaware. Their Reading Lab was based on experience stories. Each day the children were either taken to a special place or given a new experience. Then they would return and dictate a story to one of the teachers who would type it in large print. If all went according to plan, the child would then be motivated to read his story. Andrew did everything his creative mind could think of to avoid having to read his story. His favorite escape was the aquarium where he would watch the fish until forced to return to the dreaded task of reading.

At the conclusion of the summer program, I was called in for a review of his progress. "Mrs. Biasotto," a stern, middle-aged woman with an impressive number of degrees on her wall said to me, "you must accept the fact that Andrew is just not going to read as long as he has a fear of failure. He doesn't have a learning disability, but he does need psychiatric help. We recommend that you find a psychiatrist as soon as possible who can help him become unblocked." She shuffled through a stack of test results and stopped abruptly. "My goodness!" she exclaimed. "He has a remarkably high I.Q. I would never have expected that from a child so severely reading impaired. This is unusual!" She seemed to warm to me a little after that, but she still had no other suggestions.

I went home confused and upset. After dinner, I sat down in the living room with Lawrence and relayed all that the reading supervisor had told me. "I just can't believe that he needs a psychiatrist," I said soberly.

It was quiet for a while, and then Lawrence broke the silence. "If she said that's what he needs, then maybe we should get him one. She's supposed to be the expert."

"No," I shook my head. "I feel in my heart that he doesn't need that kind of help. Sure he's afraid of failing. Wouldn't you be, if everything that crossed your desk was in a foreign language? How long would it take you to quit? The sad thing is that he can't quit. He has to go to school. He has no choice. What was it that the psychologist in Ohio said? 'The smarter they are, the quicker they quit.'"

"Well, if you don't think he needs psychiatric help, what do you think we should do now? What's left?"

"I don't know," I answered glumly. "I guess we have no choice but to trust that they will teach him something in school. They are the only other experts we know. I don't know anything else to try."

Intervention

Sixth grade was just a continuation of the fifth. It was as if the Reading Clinic had never happened. Andrew's teachers were kind and motherly and expected little of him that required reading and writing. His math was above grade level and science, his favorite subject, was the brightest spot in his day. A distant cloud on the horizon was seventh grade. That meant a new school, new teachers, new friends, new enemies and new standards. I forced myself not to think about it.

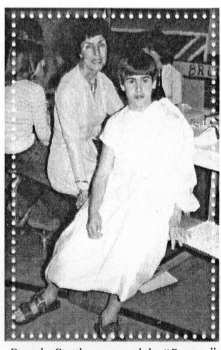

Dorothy Stottlemeyer and the "Roman"

In February, Dottie Stottlemeyer called to tell us that she was recommending an evaluation for Andrew to help with placement in junior high. He had not been given a battery of tests for three and a half years, and she felt it was time to do it again. We agreed.

Promptly at 8 a.m. we arrived for our appointment with Mr. Tom Ackerson, the school psychologist. He was a kind, friendly man, but this morning his demeanor was strained. "It took me three sessions to test Andrew because he resisted so strongly," he began. "He tried to delay my questions with questions of his own. He talked constantly and had a very hard time sitting in his chair. Finally he relaxed enough to allow me to partially test him. I'm afraid I don't have very good news."

Lawrence and I sat frozen in our seats trying to take in what we were hearing. Neither of us had expected anything serious, other than the already known problem with written language. We came thinking that the subject of the meeting was the district's recommendation of placement for 7th grade. We had not allowed ourselves to face what not being able to read was doing to our son.

"When asked to draw a picture of himself, Andrew drew a mutilated figure with his head and limbs cut off," Mr. Ackerson said as he showed us a grotesque drawing. "He feels incomplete, not a whole person."

The lump in my throat made it impossible to talk. Tears welled in my eyes as I waited for the next revelation.

"In the next test, I asked Andrew to finish a sentence that I began: 'My brother thinks' and he said, 'I am stupid.' I said 'My sister is' and he said, 'smart and pretty.' I said, 'My father is' and he said, 'a great man who works hard.' I said 'My friends' and he said, 'don't like me because I am dumb.'"

I had heard all I could stand. Of all the pain that I had felt for Andrew, this was the greatest. My husband held me and let me cry. Mr. Ackerson remained discretely silent.

When I regained my composure, Mr. Ackerson said seriously, "This is crisis time. Andrew has a seven-year gap between his mental age and his reading level. If something isn't done immediately, he will never realize his potential. I find him to be genetically dyslexic. If he were my boy, I would have this diagnosis confirmed by an outside psychologist and then send him to a school where they teach in a way appropriate to how he learns."

"Then you don't think that our school district has what he needs?" Lawrence asked him.

"I can't say that. You understand. You should look at the Intensive Learning Center before making a final decision, but if he were my boy..." His voice trailed off. "He needs the best. He has so much catching up to do."

"Would you recommend a psychologist?" Lawrence asked.

"Yes. Dr. Milton Brutten," he answered without hesitation. "If you like, I will call for an appointment for you."

We gratefully accepted and Mr. Ackerson made an appointment for the following month.

As we rose to leave, I looked at my watch. It was 11:10. We had been in Mr. Ackerson's office for over three hours. I was physically and emotionally drained. Looking at Lawrence's face, I could tell that he too, had experienced an ordeal.

There was nothing to say on the way home. Each of us was deep in his own pain. Lawrence unlocked the front door and we walked inside. "Well, what do we do now?" he asked. I walked to him and we held each other.

"We see Dr. Brutten and then…I don't know. Thank goodness I have you to lean on," I said, feeling the strength of his arms around me.

"I wish I had someone to lean on," he said quietly.

We ate lunch in silence and Lawrence left for work. The phone rang and I answered it. "Ginger, this is Mary Louise." Suddenly I remembered that I had missed teaching a neighborhood Bible study that morning. I hadn't cancelled because I thought our conference would be over in plenty of time.

"We knew something rather serious must have happened for you to miss coming, so we prayed for you. A lady, who had never come before and nobody knew, said that God gave her a scripture for you. It is Psalm 138:8. 'I will accomplish that which concerns you.' Does that make any sense to you?"

"Mary Louise, we spent the morning in the psychologist's office learning how bad things are for Andrew. That promise is a lifeline!"

I copied the verse, and then put it on the refrigerator. When I would get discouraged, and I often did, I would read that promise and, to the extent of my faith, believe.

The young woman who came to the Bible study that morning never returned, but she had brought me a message of hope. I was sorry not to be able to tell her how important that hope was to me in the years to come.

Jemicy

The drive to Dr. Brutten's office was about an hour long. Andrew chatted happily and seemed relaxed as we drove along. It was as if he sensed that we were on the right track at last.

The office was located on property that appeared to be a farm. There were horses grazing nearby and other animals in the distance. The rural setting should have helped to put me at ease, but my mind was on Andrew and all of the roads we had traveled in search of an answer to help this puzzle child.

Do I dare put my faith in the opinion of another human being? I asked myself. *Will this man be able to guide us in the right direction, or will he be just another dead-end? How could Andrew not feel defeated after trying so many things that didn't work?*

We waited in the small, dark, paneled room for what seemed like an eternity before Dr. Brutten greeted us. He was a soft-spoken, friendly man who was oblivious to my tension. He and Andrew chatted amiably, as he led him downstairs for testing. I read dozens of nature magazines before I heard their voices again. They were carrying on a lively conversation, and when he saw me, Dr. Brutten said, "Andrew tells me that you are interested in art. I have a collection of paintings that I am quite proud of." A sweep of his arm led my eye to various art objects on the wall. He continued to describe his taste in art. When he began to mention artists he felt I might know, I could stand it no longer and interrupted.

"What did you learn about Andrew?"

"Oh, Andrew and I had a fine time together. I do need another morning to finish up the testing. Make an appointment with my secretary and bring your husband with you. I'll meet with the two of you after lunch and make my recommendations."

As we left Dr. Brutten's office, I felt resentment. *This man was more interested in his art collection than he was in my son. How could he make cocktail party conversation in what to me was a life and death situation?* My initial impression of this psychologist was that he was a very superficial individual with little concern about Andrew. How very wrong I was.

Before the second meeting with Dr. Brutten, I researched all of the private schools in the Philadelphia area that specialized in teaching learning disabled children. There were two that were an hour from our home that seemed likely choices. Dr. Brutten was the head of another school for children with a variety of severe problems. It seemed possible that Dr. Brutten might recommend his school. In any case, it looked like I was going to be on the road most of the day, as a result of the long commute. That posed a problem because I wanted to be home when Kara and Larry were out of school, but they would just have to take care of each other. *Maybe*, I thought, *I should get a job near the school so that I would only have to drive two hours a day instead of four.* All of those thoughts were swirling around in my head. I have never dealt well with the unknown, and there were many huge question marks in our future.

The three of us had a silent ride to Dr. Brutten's office. After a short wait, Andrew happily went with Dr. Brutten for the rest of his testing and Lawrence joined me in flipping through the nature magazines stacked on the tables. Finally it was our turn to follow Dr. Brutten down the narrow stairway to his office.

The room that housed his desk was unpretentious. I noted more art treasures hanging on the wall, toys on the floor, and stacks of papers on his desk.

Dr. Brutten began. "First of all I would like you to know that Mr. Ackerson's report was completely accurate, and I concur with all he said. Andrew is genetically dyslexic, a child in trouble. Unless he is sent to a school where he can be quickly remediated, he will never hope to reach his potential."

As I listened to his words, my thoughts went to the schools that I had researched, and I waited for him to mention one of them or perhaps his school as the best place for Andrew to go.

Dr. Brutten continued. "There are six schools in the world good enough for Andrew at this point."

I held my breath. *Did he say, "In the world"?*

"There's a fine school in California that is appropriate," he continued.

I gasped and Dr. Brutten, sensing my distress, skipped over the next four schools and then gave us what he felt would be good news. "Actually, the one I would most like to see him attend is close to home."

Here it comes, I thought. *Here is where he will recommend his school.*

"The Jemicy School in Owings Mills, Maryland is only six years old, but they have an excellent program for dyslexics like Andrew. It is not a boarding school, which does present a problem, but I would like you to see the school as soon as you can. Andrew has no time to waste."

I was in shock. All of my mental arrangements for commuting to Philadelphia were suddenly out the window, and I was faced with a situation for which I had no mental picture. In desperation I asked about the two schools I had researched.

"Not suitable," Dr. Brutten said definitely. "Neither focuses on the dyslexic child. Their populations include children with a wide variety of disabilities. Andrew's needs are specific."

"Well, what about your school?" I asked in desperation, hardly believing my own words. Ten minutes before I was mentally daring him to suggest it as a placement for Andrew.

"Andrew must have a challenging academic environment with daily tutoring in the Orton-Gillingham approach. He will get both of those at Jemicy. My school cannot provide the reading training he must have."

Dr. Brutten spent the rest of the time reviewing test results. I tried to focus on what he was saying, but my mind drifted to an unknown school in a small town on the outskirts of Baltimore, Maryland. So many questions were running through my head. *How can he possibly go when it isn't a boarding school? Can we let our twelve-year old leave home? Where will he live? What is this Orton-Gillingham approach?*

As we walked to the car, I was aware for the first time of my husband's discomfort. He looked at me and shook his head. "There is no way I can send Andrew away. There's got to be another solution."

"But Dr. Brutten didn't give us any other way," I reminded him. "We know that Delaware doesn't have a school for dyslexic children and from what he just said, neither does the Philadelphia area. I don't want him to go away any more than you do, but I don't see any alternative."

Lawrence looked grim as he started the car. For several miles, no one spoke. Finally he looked at Andrew in the rear view mirror. "The doctor says that you need to go to a school near Baltimore. Your mother and I don't want you to go. What do you think?"

"Well, dad, it might be an interesting experience."

"You mean you would be willing to go away from home?" Lawrence asked his son in surprise.

"If I have to go, I'll go," Andrew answered.

Lawrence caught my eye and the expression on his face revealed a mixture of pride and amazement.

As soon as we returned home, I dialed the number Dr. Brutten had given us and made an appointment to visit the Jemicy School on May 11, 1978. At my request they promised to send us information about the school. When it arrived a few days later, I was disappointed. Instead of the sophisticated, glossy booklet I was expecting from a private school, what arrived were a few sheets of mimeographed paper. I learned a few details, including tuition, but little else. *Strike one*, I thought.

Kindnesses

On May 10th, the night before we were to visit Jemicy, I announced at the dinner table that I was going to the local high school to hear Bill Glass speak. He had been a professional football player who felt the call to become a Christian Evangelist. When I asked if anyone would like to come with me, only Andrew responded. After doing the dishes, he and I set out for the school.

Neither of us had ever been to a revival meeting, so we didn't know what to expect. I was tired and although the service was very inspiring, I looked forward to a good night's sleep before driving to the Jemicy School the next day.

Bill Glass based his message on Luke 8:5-15, the sower and the seed. "If you have ears to hear, hear and respond," he said to the people in the auditorium.

I felt warm and happy sitting there listening to those age-old words. Seven years before, I had responded to the call of Christ and it had changed my life. It was good to be sharing this with Andrew.

"If you hear my words and feel God pulling you, don't resist. Come forward and publicly declare your faith in Jesus Christ."

Andrew nudged me. "I'm going," he said, and before I had

a chance to reply, he was out of his seat and walking toward the stage. I felt a brief moment of frustration. My plan had been to make a quick exit in order to get out of the parking lot ahead of the crowd. Now it appeared that we would be one of the last. *That's a small price to pay,* my heart reminded me.

Bill Glass stooped down and leaned over the edge of the stage to talk to Andrew. It was impossible to determine what he was saying, and as others came forward, I lost sight of my son. When we met 45 minutes later in the lobby, Andrew was carrying a new Bible. My emotions were extreme. I was joyful to know that Andrew had made the most important decision of his life, but I felt sad that he couldn't read the Bible he was carrying. *He belongs to God,* I thought, *and tomorrow we go to Jemicy!*

The drive to Baltimore seemed to take forever. Each of us was engrossed in his own thoughts. I let my mind drift over the past seven years. We had lived in New Jersey, Maryland, California, Ohio and Delaware. We had tried to solve Andrew's reading problem with physical exercises, behavior modification, constant tutoring, reading clinics, Ritalin, developmental lenses and the Feingold diet. Nothing had worked. Now we were on our way to what very well may be our last chance…a school where other children with reading and spelling problems were being helped by a method called "Orton-Gillingham." I glanced over at Lawrence. His eyes were firmly fixed on the road ahead of him and there was no way to read his thoughts. Andrew, too, was unusually quiet.

That poor kid, I thought. *He has been yanked from pillar to post, subjected to testing of every kind, experimented on from the east coast to the west coast and back again. He has been abused by those he would like to call friends. Surely this baptism by fire had to have an end!*

"What exit do I take off the beltway?" Lawrence's question penetrated my thoughts. I checked the map and gave him directions. Soon we found ourselves on a beautiful country road heading for the Jemicy School. We passed several magnificent estates and my expectations began to rise. Perhaps the school was going to be nice despite the lack of glossy fliers.

"The directions say to turn left at the bottom of this hill onto Velvet Way," I instructed. "Then take the first left. Jemicy School is at the end of that street."

We all felt a great sense of excitement as we approached the school. It appeared to be an old dairy barn with a modern wing added to it. The outside looked friendly, and I realized that I wanted with all my being to like this school.

We parked the car and walked to what appeared to be the entrance. Two large dogs lazily got up, stretched, and wagged their tails as we approached. "Well, the dogs seem to like us," said Lawrence. "Maybe that's a good sign."

Andrew petted both dogs thoroughly, and then we walked through the front door of Jemicy School. My preconceived notions of a private school included shining woodwork and an environment of subdued elegance. What I saw was a huge black dog sprawled on thread-bear carpeting. Dust balls in the corners and the remains of muddy footprints trailing down the hall. *Strike two.*

While mentally trying to adapt to this new disappointment, I watched Andrew take off ahead of us. We stepped carefully around the dog and followed him. By the time we got to the office, he was happily chatting with the secretary. I noted that the office was just an extension of the hall. My mind flipped back to the mimeographed sheets that had come in the mail. They fit perfectly into this setting.

"Her name is Barbara," Andrew informed us, nodding toward the secretary. We smiled, and Barbara extended her hand warmly while telling us that David Malin, the headmaster, was teaching a class. Soon he would be free to show us around the school. It had been arranged for Andrew to be paired with a student for the day. We would see him again at lunch.

Barbara took us to David's office. It had a door that kept a dog inside who wasn't terribly glad to see us. He was a Maltese who discouraged petting.

The bell rang, and in a few minutes the door opened and a slim young man with sandy hair and a neatly trimmed beard was standing before us. We introduced ourselves and I was distinctly aware that he seemed momentarily to have forgotten that we were coming.

"Oh, yes. The Biasottos from Delaware. Your son is Andrew," he reminded himself.

"Yes," Lawrence confirmed. "We have come from Wilmington. Dr. Brutten recommended your school."

"Well, I have a few minutes. Let me show you around," David offered.

The tour of Jemicy was a bombardment to my senses. I am not a fastidious housekeeper, by any means, but I had an overwhelming desire to find their vacuum cleaner, if they had one, and start at one end of the school and work toward the other. Every classroom had shelves piled with projects. Artwork and science projects lined the corridors. There was a flurry of activity everywhere we went, but there was no disorder. I commented to David that the children all seemed to know what they were doing. His response impressed me. "Sometimes I think that if none of the teachers showed up, the school would run just as well because the children all know what they are supposed to be doing at all times. They have freedom within the structure, but they know the structure."

The last morning class was over, and we went to the office to wait for Andrew. I saw him at the end of the hall talking to another boy. When he saw us, he ran in our direction, his face shining in excitement. Before we had a chance to ask him about his morning, he blurted out, "Mom, Dad! This is the most wonderful school in the world! Nobody puts you down!"

Homerun! Suddenly, the dust balls in the corners began to shrink. In a flash, it struck me that the Jemicy School was a reflection of Andrew. Dust never bothered him. Every room in our house had some kind of project that Andrew was working on. He was a whirlwind of activity just as these children in the classrooms were. I looked at our happy son and silently vowed that we would make it possible for him to attend this school, even if I had to come to Baltimore and live in a tent.

"Dad, you should see the science room. The teacher, his name is Joe, was explaining about a Fresnel lens. I was the only person who knew what it was. I think Joe likes me, Dad. He stayed after class and showed me all the stuff. Joe's really neat, Dad!"

"That's great, son, but do you think you should call the teacher by his first name?"

"Everybody does, Dad. All the teachers go by their first names."

I could tell that Lawrence didn't approve. We had both been raised to show respect for authority, and adults were always known as Mr. or Mrs. If children and teachers all went by first names, wouldn't that detract from the respect that a child should show his teacher?

I voiced this question to David Malin later. His answer satisfied both of us.

"When children come to Jemicy, they have usually been subjected to humiliation and put downs and have very poor self images. We feel that if everyone is on a first name basis, then it will help the children gain some self respect because they are being put on a par with their teachers."

It made sense. Certainly there was no evidence of lack of respect for the teachers. If anything, the children seemed to exhibit great affection and camaraderie that isn't generally seen in schools.

The dust balls were now practically invisible!

Before leaving Jemicy, David Malin gave Andrew a test to determine in a general way what he knew about phonics. When he finished, he sent Andrew outside to watch lacrosse practice and then returned to talk to us.

"Andrew has some skills, but many holes. In order to be able to read, he must have a strict adherence to the Orton-Gillingham approach. Some children can have a little of it mixed with other reading instruction. Andrew must have every skill in order to be able to decode words. He is more severely impaired than most of our students and certainly has the greatest distance to catch up. It is my recommendation that you consider a boarding school where he can have 24-hour supervision and instruction. A school like the Kildonan School would be better for Andrew than the Jemicy School. I'm not saying flat out that we won't take him, but he needs the best and I'm not sure our day school will be enough. Think about it."

I felt sick to my stomach. During the course of the day, we had all become convinced that Jemicy was the place for Andrew. The main reason was Andrew's enthusiasm. After all, he was going to be the one to sacrifice by leaving home. We wanted him to learn and be happy, and by all indications, he would be both at Jemicy. Of course, the prime consideration was remediation. What should we do? What should we do? My head ached.

Lawrence and I were quiet on the drive home, but Andrew filled the void with a steady stream of chatter. He had found a home away from home, or at least that's what he thought. Where he would live was not an issue for him. His words played themselves over and over in my mind. *This is the most wonderful school in the world. Nobody puts you down.*

After dinner, I called Dr. Brutten to report on our visit to Jemicy. It was, after all, his recommendation that sent us there and he should have something to say about David Malin's concerns.

He listened to my long discourse. When I had finished, he told me not to worry. Jemicy School was the right place for Andrew and he would call David in the morning and convince him that Andrew should be accepted. I felt as if a weight had been lifted. Dr. Brutten's decisiveness enabled me to sleep that night. He was orchestrating Andrew's future and I was beyond grateful.

Listening

"The question before us is do we have an appropriate placement for Andrew Biasotto in the New Castle County School District?" the psychologist, Tom Ackerson, said to the members of the committee.

Lawrence and I sat quietly listening to the discussion of teachers and administrators who were responsible for creating his Individual Education Plan (IEP). Since 1976, Senate Bill 94-142 gave parents the right to insist on an appropriate education for exceptional children who could not learn within the traditional classroom setting. If the school could provide Andrew with an appropriate educational plan, then we needed to know what it was before making a definite decision to send him to the Jemicy School.

Dorothy Stottlemeyer reviewed Andrew's background for those present who didn't know him. She explained how, in spite of daily tutoring by the reading specialist for four years, Andrew was struggling to read on a second grade level. His spelling was so poor that the test results were off the chart. His handwriting was illegible. Math, on the other hand, was on grade level, and Andrew could discuss science on a level far beyond his 12 years.

"How can we be sure that a low I.Q. isn't responsible for his poor performance in school?" interjected Mr. Campbell, the assistant to the Superintendent. "If Andrew has been given all this extra help and is still so far behind, then perhaps he just isn't as bright as his parents seem to think he is, or maybe he is a bit lazy and just doesn't want to put out the effort necessary to learn."

I cringed inwardly and felt Lawrence's anger as he shifted in his seat. How many times had I been guilty of telling him to try harder? Dr. Brutten had helped us realize that trying harder would never teach Andrew to read.

Lawrence started to speak, but Mr. Ackerson quieted him with a move of his hand. "I can tell you unequivocally that Andrew is well above average, probably superior," he began. "His I.Q. test in the third grade indicated a score of 133. Because he had experienced three years of school failure before that, I expect it was even higher. Each year since then it has gone down and on the last test I gave him, he scored 112. Considering the terrible tension he was experiencing while taking the test, I am quite sure that a true score would place him at least 20—25 points higher. This boy would undoubtedly be a candidate for the gifted program if he were not dyslexic."

Mrs. Stottlemeyer leaned toward Mr. Campbell. "Let me tell you about a recent experience I had with Andrew. Each year I take my 5th graders to the historic Brandywine Battlefield. Last year, Andrew was in the group. He asked good questions and had a marvelous time. This year, I asked him if he would like to go back with the 5th graders and see it again. He said he would. The same guide took us through the museum. As she talked to the group, Andrew reminded her of facts that she left out which she had mentioned the year before. He remembered everything she had said and afterwards discussed it with her. She said to me as we were leaving, 'I have never met a child with such a phenomenal memory. He must be a genius!'" Mrs. Stottlemeyer paused. "Mr. Campbell, Andrew has a seven year gap between his reading level and his mental age. He is a child in great trouble."

There was silence in the room. Finally Mr. Campbell spoke. "What would you propose for us to do for him next year? What do you think is appropriate?" He directed the question to all of us in the room.

Tom Ackerson spoke up. "The Intensive Learning Center is a new concept in the district. It is the only thing that would be appropriate. There are two teachers for 8-10 children. He would get plenty of individualized help. At the present time there is a class existing in the junior high school. Perhaps Mr. and Mrs. Biasotto would like to observe the class and speak to the teachers about Andrew."

"Do they provide Orton-Gillingham instruction?" I asked.

"I don't know," Tom replied. "You would have to ask them."

"How do we know that this Orton-Gillingham method is really what Andrew needs?" questioned Mr. Campbell. "What makes it any better than what he already has had?"

This time Lawrence answered. "Dr. Milton Brutten told us that this was the right approach for Andrew, and Mr. Ackerson also concurred in his report. The Jemicy School has recommended that Andrew attend their summer school and begin training. If it is right for Andrew, then we should know by the end of the summer."

"Then why don't we delay making a decision about placement until after he finishes summer school?" Dottie Stottlemeyer suggested. "If he makes progress, then we will know that this is something he must have."

"Is that agreeable to you?" Tom Ackerson looked in our direction. I looked at Lawrence and he nodded. "Fine. We will set another meeting for the beginning of August."

As we rose to leave, Tom Ackerson said quietly to us, "I still think it would be a good idea for you to visit the Intensive Learning Center while it is still in session."

"Mr. Ackerson wants to see Andrew go to Jemicy," Lawrence said on the way home.

"How can you tell?" I asked. "He seemed supportive of his school's program and quite objective."

"It's his job to represent the school district, but I think that personally he feels Andrew's best shot is outside the system."

Lawrence had a way of evaluating people and situations that I didn't have. He seemed to be gifted with a sixth sense that enabled him to make job decisions based on very little information. I had learned that he could read people and he was usually right. He was right this time, too.

Mission

"I made an appointment with the teacher in charge of the Intensive Learning Center," I announced at breakfast. "I'm going to sit in for a few hours this morning and try to get a feel for their program."

"It's good you did that," Lawrence said as he finished his toast. "Mr. Ackerson has a reason for wanting you to go, and I'd like to know what it is."

Classes were changing as I entered the junior high school. Boys and girls were hurrying from lockers to classrooms. Greetings and jokes were exchanged freely and I noted what a happy place this school seemed to be.

In the office, I was given directions to the Intensive Learning Center and hurriedly made my way around groups of teens using the last available minute to socialize before going into their classes.

It must be the next room, I said to myself, counting the classrooms. Sure enough, there was a large sign on the door. INTENSIVE LEARNING CENTER. Youthful hands from the junior high had decorated the sign with their own interpretations.

"Looney bin", "stupids", "retards", "dummy class", "weirdoes", "idiots" and other insulting words jumped out at me. For several moments I stared at the sign, disbelieving. It had been hanging there for some time. The graffiti was not new. The boys and girls in this class were subjected to these demeaning slurs every time they entered or left their room. I wondered if any of the happy smiling teenagers I passed in the hall had a hand in decorating this sign.

Anger rose in me. Anger for the teacher who allowed this terrible sign to stay posted on the door and anger against the small, uncaring minds that put down others who were different from themselves. I took a deep breath and knocked on the door.

A tall boy with a vacant look in his eyes let me in. The teacher waved me to a seat in the back of the room and motioned that she would join me shortly. My entry had interrupted the work of several students, and they stared at me in bored distraction. I looked over the group of children to see if I could see any children who reminded me of Andrew. None did.

The teacher finished what she was doing and walked back to me. Pulling up a chair she said, "I don't know how they expect us to teach these kids. You see Joey over there? He hasn't said a word in over a year. Martha is deaf, but she has a good mind. Brad is truly a mental case. Sometimes he goes berserk and the whole class falls apart."

"Are there any learning disabled children here?" I asked hesitantly.

"One," she said. "He's doing a math sheet. There's nothing wrong with him except that he is way behind in reading."

I looked at the small blond boy sitting alone in the back of the room. He was looking out the window. Every once in a while he would refocus his eyes on the paper before him and write down an answer.

"He's a good kid," said the teacher, watching my gaze. "Bright, too. I wish all these children were as normal as he is. It would make my life a lot easier."

"How do you teach him? Reading, I mean."

She brightened. "Experience stories mostly. Of course we use phonics, too. He'll never be a good reader, but he's coming along."

"You said he's bright. What do you do to challenge his mind?"

"That's a real problem here," she answered. "Since he can't read very well, I can't give him reports to do on his own and no one else in the class can work in a group with him. We have been promised a computer, and when we get it, he will be able to use that independently. But for now he does a lot of workbook sheets and experiences one on one teaching with me or my assistant. I know it's not good, but it's the best that we can do."

I pictured Jemicy. What a contrast between this classroom and the stimulating, happy school we had recently visited. Suddenly, I felt sorry for this teacher who had been charged with educating eight children with totally different handicaps. She was doing her best, but I vowed at that moment that I would die before I let my child be buried in this hopeless cave.

As I got up to leave, my eyes met the gaze of the little blond boy in the back of the room. I could leave, but he had to stay. His eyes seemed to ask, "And what are you going to do for me?"

Nancy

"Don't worry, Mrs. Biasotto. Miracles happen here everyday!" Barbara's words reminded me of the promise that God had given me. *I will accomplish that which concerns you.* At this moment, that which concerned me was a place for Andrew to stay while going to summer school at Camp Bombadil, the Jemicy School summer program. David Malin had agreed to admit Andrew in the fall if he came to summer school and responded well to his Orton-Gillingham training. People drove their children for many miles to attend this program, but an eighty-mile commute from Delaware was out of the question.

"Someone will take him in. Don't worry. It will all work out. You'll see." Barbara's voice was reassuring, and I felt a sense of optimism as I hung up the phone.

A call from David Malin several days later proved that Barbara had been right. The Benfers' son Keith was also going to attend Bombadil. They had agreed to let Andrew board with them over the summer. Their home was in the country with few children Keith's age nearby, and they thought Andrew would be good company for Keith.

We gratefully contacted the Benfers and made arrangements to bring Andrew to their home on the day before camp started.

We found them a warm, loving couple who welcomed Andrew with open arms. They showed him Keith's room that he was to share. "The boys will be great friends," they said enthusiastically. What no one put into this equation was Keith's feelings. As time passed, it became clear that he was not thrilled to have to share his room, his parents, his grandparents and his possessions with a stranger. To make matters worse, their personalities clashed and fighting was the rule of the day. "They argue about everything," Mrs. Benfer told me later. "Driving them to and from camp is a nightmare because neither will let the other have the last word."

There was nothing we could do except relieve them on the weekends and hope that Andrew and Keith would come to some kind of a truce. Mercifully, the seven weeks passed without any bodily harm coming to either boy.

On the last day of the camp, we met with David Malin and Nancy Simonetti, Andrew's tutor. Nancy was a tall, gray-haired, middle-aged woman with a very kind face. When she spoke, I had to strain to hear the softly spoken words. How Andrew must have liked being with such a gentle soul.

"Nancy is our dean of tutors," David told us. "We assigned Andrew to her because of her experience and unthreatening manner. Andrew has been through so much that he needs to be with someone like Nancy." He turned to her. "Nancy, please tell the Biasottos how Andrew did with you."

"We need to know how he responded to the Orton-Gillingham training," Lawrence spoke up before Nancy had a chance to reply.

"For the first two weeks Andrew used every stalling tactic he knew," she began seriously. "He talked about everything under the sun to try to avoid the task before him, but then in the third week, a change occurred. He began to trust me and to trust the system. This report will enable you to see exactly what we accomplished, but I can tell you that he is learning by this approach. It is vital that he continue in the fall."

I wanted to reach across the table and hug her. It was working! What she and Andrew did together was working! Nancy had just told us that he must have Orton-Gillingham training because through this approach he was learning to read. The gray cloud we had been living under for so long was lifting. If our public school couldn't provide this for our son, Jemicy could. In my mind, Jemicy was a done deal. *Now, Barbara*, I thought, *just one more miracle please…a place for Andrew to live in the fall.*

Orton-Gillingham

Lawrence was still having a hard time with the idea of sending Andrew to a school away from home. He felt that if there was any chance that the local school system could provide an appropriate program, we should seriously consider it. He agreed with me that the Intensive Learning Center was out, but our final meeting with Mr. Ackerson, Mrs. Stottlemeyer and the other members of the committee hadn't been held yet. Surely the thing to do was to meet with them again, present the results of the summer school program, and then find out if there was anyone who could teach him by the Orton-Gillingham approach in our public school system.

After trying for two weeks to get the committee to meet, I finally gave up. It seemed as though everyone was taking a vacation in August. Only one administrator was available, and it was finally decided that we would meet with him. Even though he hadn't been present at the first meeting, he would be responsible for putting together an IEP.

We filled him in on what had occurred at the first meeting and then presented the report from Nancy Simonetti. At the conclusion of the meeting, he turned over the paper on which he had been taking notes and wrote out an IEP for Andrew. *Put him in average ability classes so that he will have some mental stimulation and tell his teachers not to expect him to read or write.*

When he presented it to us, we were stunned. One of the side effects of Andrew's dyslexia was a low self esteem from years of failing, and this IEP would not help to raise it. On the contrary, exclusion in the area of reading and writing would only make him feel less and less able. In addition, no provision had been made for teaching him to read. The district had given us a Band-aid for a broken leg!

In a strange way, it was a relief. The situation was clearly black and white. There was no doubt in my mind that Andrew should go to Jemicy, but Lawrence wanted to be absolutely sure that there were no teachers in the junior high school who could teach the Orton-Gillingham approach.

The next day, I made one last phone call before sending in the tuition payment for Andrew's first semester at the Jemicy School. It was to the reading specialist. "Do you know the Orton-Gillingham approach?" I asked her.

"Orton-Gilling-what?" she asked.

I repeated the name and she said, "I've never heard of it, but I'll ask around and see if I can find anyone who does."

I never heard from her again.

Passage

Once the decision had been made, it felt as if a gigantic weight had been lifted. Then Barbara's second miracle happened when Nancy Simonetti invited Andrew to live with her family! We liked Nancy and her twin daughters, Regina and Claudia, who had also worked with Andrew in the camp. It was a tremendous relief to know that our son would be in the home of such good and caring people.

School started in two weeks. We spent the time collecting the materials David told us Andrew would need and getting his clothes in order.

The day that we were to take Andrew to Baltimore finally arrived. The atmosphere in the car on the trip down was tense. I knew that Lawrence was having a difficult time. Releasing his twelve-year-old son to virtual strangers in a distant city was hard. Family came first with him, and in the past he was always able to provide anything his family needed. Now, he was helpless and on the receiving end of the generosity of others. I, too, was having trouble becoming a taker. Not only is it better to give than to receive, it is also easier.

We followed Nancy's directions, exiting on Charles Street, passing the Cathedral and finally turning onto Upnor Road.

"There it is. Number 210," Andrew said. Lawrence eased the car over to the curb and shut off the engine. Andrew opened the back door and hopped out while Lawrence and I hung back. Neither of us wanted to leave its familiarity. "Well, this is it," Lawrence said with resignation. "Let's go."

Andrew led the way to the front door and rang the doorbell. We were met by Claudia and Regina, who politely invited us inside. They were quiet girls and I wondered how they would react to Andrew's constant chatter.

Nancy called from the kitchen and the three of us went back to greet her. Andrew discovered the game, *Simon*, and was busily pushing its buttons creating a musical background for our conversation. Nancy's husband Bob, we were told, had been delayed at the bank, but he would be home as soon as he could. Naturally, we would wait dinner until he arrived.

Andrew disappeared with the twins to inspect his new room and I used the time to fill Nancy in on some of his food preferences. "He will eat anything, but really enjoys orange juice best for a drink, especially in the morning," I began.

Nancy wrote down, "Buy orange juice."

"He's used to fixing himself a bowl of Raisin Bran, so don't feel that you have to get his breakfast. Peanut butter and jelly is fine for lunch." There were so many things I wanted to say, but I suddenly realized that I was attempting to pass on my role as mother to Nancy. Twelve years of getting to know Andrew could not be shared in a few minutes. She would have to learn for herself.

Dinner was a very pleasant affair. The Biasotto side of the table did most of the talking. I wondered again how the intrusion of a new person would affect the Simonetti family.

After dinner, Andrew took us upstairs to see his room. It really belonged to Peter, the Simonettis' son who had recently left for college. If the room reflected Peter's personality, he was a contrast to his sisters. The walls were orange. The woodwork was orange and the bedspread was orange. I shut my eyes for a moment to get some relief from the intensity of color. If Andrew was aware of this unusual feature of his *new* room, he didn't show it. He plopped on the bed and declared it comfortable. He showed me where the twins had put his clothes away. He wandered around inspecting the things that Peter left behind. There was no doubt about it. Andrew had moved in and was ready to begin his new adventure. I swallowed, feeling a rather large lump in my throat. *Don't you dare be sad*, I told myself. *Count yourself blessed that Andrew's attitude is so positive. If he didn't want to be here, we'd probably take him home and he would never learn to read.*

My musings were interrupted by Lawrence's voice. "It's getting late. We probably should go." We expressed our gratitude to the Simonettis once again and headed for the door.

"Well, boy," Lawrence said to Andrew. "It's time to go. We'll pick you up at the train station on Friday night. Work hard and help out whenever you can." He hugged his son. I didn't say anything, but waited my turn. I put my arms around him and held him for a long time. Many thoughts went through my mind. *Truly this is our last hope. He knows it, too. These next two years will determine the direction for the rest of his life.*

Return

In most families the first day of school is special. Pictures are taken, new clothes are worn and pencils and notebooks are new and shiny. I wasn't there, but I knew some of that was happening for Andrew. Back in Wilmington, Larry and Kara were each getting ready to go to a new school. They were excited, and I poured my energies into getting them prepared. Then, the day before school was to start, the teachers went on strike. Classrooms were empty, picket lines went up, and children sat in front of television sets. I was grateful all over again that the decision to send Andrew to Jemicy had been made and he was in school and learning.

Each night at dinner we talked about Andrew. It was all I could do not to call, but we had to watch our spending. Tuition, room and board had taken a large bite out of our savings.

When Friday finally arrived, I could hardly wait for five o'clock when his train was due. The traffic was heavy and rain was falling as I drove through the city to the train station, but no amount of gloom could dampen my spirits. Five long days had passed since I had seen my child and I couldn't wait. Questions flooded by mind. *When do you get up? How long does it take to drive to Jemicy? Tell me about your classes. What about your teachers? Are they nice? Are you learning lots? What sport do you play after school? Were you homesick? What does Nancy feed you?* The list went on and on. I felt a need to have a detailed picture of his new life.

Once the car was parked, I hurried up the steps and into the train station. I was early and the train was late. Sitting down, I stared at the clock, willing the hands to move more quickly. Finally, I heard the announcement that I had been waiting for. People meeting passengers were supposed to wait downstairs, but I slipped by the uniformed train official and ran up the steps. Men and women in business suits were disembarking. My eyes scanned the crowd looking for a little boy with a suitcase. Suddenly I saw him. My vision blurred and at the same time an enormous grin spread across my face. I wanted to push through the people, grab him and hold on, but I limited myself to a wave. *Restrain yourself, Ginger. Don't get overly emotional. For his sake, keep it light.*

"Hi, Mom." He gave me a brief hug and started down the steps. We didn't say anything as we walked through the train station to the car. Once we were on our way, he asked about Larry and Kara. When I told him about the teacher's strike, he didn't comment. I wondered what he was thinking.

For a while, we drove in silence. Then I said, "Andrew, we missed you."

"I missed you, too."

"Was everything all right? I mean…tell me about your days." I peeled off my questions.

"I don't know when I get up. It's not too long to Jemicy. My classes are OK. Math is easy. Joe is great. I'm goalie in soccer.

Nancy cooks okay except for tuna casserole. I hate tuna casserole!" It appeared my picture of his week would look more like a sketch.

Larry and Kara were only moderately excited to see him. I had expected them to be waiting at the front door, but instead I had to go and find them to tell them that their brother was home.

For the entire weekend, Lawrence and I focused on Andrew. It was a very unbalanced situation, and Kara soon became resentful of all of the attention he was receiving. We tried to act like his presence was a normal event, but Sunday was coming and we were trying to cram a week's worth of love into two days.

The extent of Kara's resentment became apparent on Sunday night at the train station. When she asked to go with us, I was initially pleased that she was finally showing sisterly support of her brother. Again the train was late, and as we waited, I was aware that Andrew was hurting. His chin was crinkled and he was fighting back the tears.

I thought, *It isn't fair. His sister and brother have no learning problems and can stay at home, while he has to go to a strange place all by himself.* I put my arm around his shoulders and made encouraging noises. "The time will pass quickly. Everything is going to be all right. Before you know it, you'll be back here next Friday."

Kara had had all she could stand. She glared at him and stormed, "I wish you would stay there forever! I don't like it when you are home. Mom and Dad just care about you!"

I wanted to clamp my hand over her mouth. My head knew that jealousy had gotten the upper hand and she really didn't mean her words, but my heart was in pain for Andrew, who had never asked to be the center of our attention.

"Kara, that's a terrible thing to say," I reproved her.

Instead of backing down with an apology, she came at him again with hot, angry words. "I'm glad you're going back to Baltimore!"

Andrew didn't respond. His chin was still crinkled, but I felt that he was hurting from more than Kara's words.

His train was called and we three walked slowly up the stairs. Kara and I watched as he got on the train and found a seat by the window. I touched the glass and he touched it from his side, meeting my fingers. Two big tears rolled down his cheeks, and this time I thought I would choke on the lump in my throat.

Kara had become very quiet, but she suddenly walked over to the window and knocked. Andrew looked at her and she smiled and began playing "stones, scissors, paper" with him. He played along. As the train pulled out, Kara ran along the side until its speed left her behind.

We drove home in silence. Part of me was with a frightened little boy sitting alone on a train to Baltimore. The other part wanted to reassure the child sitting beside me. *Dear, Lord,* I prayed silently. *This is so hard. How can I help Kara to understand that she is loved just as much as her brother is?* I knew that it would be futile to explain to her once again the reasons for our concern about Andrew. Jealousy is not a rational emotion and even though she loved her brother, the feelings that gripped her were honest ones.

I reached out and took her hand, hoping that physical touch would soften her spirit. "It was a kind thing to help your brother take his mind off leaving us," I began. "Did you see him smile when you started playing that game?" Silence. "I know you think it is unfair of your dad and me to give so much of our time and attention to your brother. As time goes by, we will all get used to this new arrangement for our family. Right now he is hurting and when our children hurt, we hurt. I hope you will forgive us for hurting you. We love you so much."

"It's OK, Mom. I was acting like a jerk." She squeezed my hand and we both laughed. I felt greatly relieved that, at least for now, the barrier was down.

The pain from our separation lasted most of the week. I couldn't get his crinkled chin and those two tears out of my mind. *Was he unhappy every day? Was he homesick?*

The train pulled in on time the next Friday and I was right there on the platform to meet it. "Hi," I said brightly, as Andrew hopped down from the step. "Let me help you carry some of your stuff." This time Andrew chatted easily about a man he met on the train, and as we reached the door, I turned to him and asked, "Remember how bad you felt last Sunday when you left?" He nodded. "How long did it take for you to get over feeling sad?"

"Well," he said thoughtfully, "I guess until the train pulled out of the station."

"OK, mister," I laughed. "No more tears on Sunday night. I was sad until Wednesday!"

Lawrence and I made an effort to treat Andrew normally during the weekend. When Larry and Kara were out of earshot, like vultures, we plied him with questions. We learned that he was having some positive experiences and liked the Simonettis very much. He told us about the twins and things that were going on in their lives, the conversations they had at dinner (Nancy told me later that dinner had always been a quiet affair in their household until Andrew came to live with them), and his feelings about the teachers at Jemicy.

Roger Shaw, one of his favorite teachers, had been a college professor who was looking for a change of pace. Jemicy proved to be exactly right for Roger, who gained the respect of the boys immediately. Mark Westerfelt was young and enthusiastic. He enjoyed math and imparted that love to his students. Joyce Steeves challenged him in English. She virtually ignored the fact that her students were dyslexic and gave them reading and writing assignments that stretched them to their limits. Joe Chitchester, the science teacher, was a legend in his own time. He had been an engineer working for a large corporation, and, like Roger, had decided to get out of the rat race. Jemicy gave him a home, literally. Joe slept on the couch in the teacher's room at night and challenged his students by day. He demonstrated all lessons with hands on activities. The boys made planes to learn about aerodynamics, and projects lined the shelves in the cluttered science room. No idea was ever rejected out of hand, and Joe spent long hours guiding the boys in how to prove or disprove their hypotheses. Andrew loved Joe! He was a person who listened and believed in his students. Class was fun! I couldn't wait to meet this amazing man.

School

After making the decision to send Andrew to the Jemicy School, we filed for a Due Process Hearing. This legal procedure stemmed from Senate Bill 94-142 (The Education of all Handicapped Children Act, 1975). Its purpose was to determine whether or not the school system had fulfilled its obligation to provide Andrew with an adequate education. They were charged by law to prove that they had, but in reality, we were the ones who had to prove that they had not.

Our hearing was scheduled for mid-November. Lawrence and I had been advised to act as our own lawyers. It was understood that if we didn't bring an attorney, the district wouldn't either. That proved to be the case.

Since early summer, I had been questioning those people in the school system who knew Andrew best. Then I would go home and type up their statements. Whenever there was a meeting, I took minutes carefully and typed them at home. Dr. Brutten and Mr. Ackerson's reports were the strongest statements we had, but Lawrence thought that the more opinions we could gather, the better.

The tension surrounding our upcoming hearing was very great. We knew that very few people who had taken this step had won. We had one shot at convincing the hearing officer that Andrew was "rare or complex" and we wanted to do everything right.

When the letter arrived telling us the name of the hearing officer, we felt optimistic because he was from out-of-state. Because of our experience at the University of Delaware's Reading Clinic, we knew that many educators didn't recognize the term *dyslexia*, and therefore, didn't acknowledge a way for its remediation. It appeared that *dyslexia* was an inflammatory term that divided educators right down the middle. I frankly didn't care what they called it, just as long as they understood that those children who struggle to read need special instruction that is compatible with the way their brains are wired.

The Orton-Gillingham approach was working for Andrew. Since we had tried so many things that didn't work, I was very curious to learn more about this reading approach. That opportunity arrived early one morning with a phone call. The voice on the line said, "Hello, I'm Alice Koontz. Nancy Simonetti told me that you are interested in learning about the Orton-Gillingham approach, and I'm calling to tell you about a class I'm teaching near you." I blinked and sat up on the edge of the bed, trying to take in all she was saying. "We've met once already, but if you are interested, I can catch you up. The class is on Friday nights and all day Saturday at Villanova University."

I stuttered a few stalling words. "That's very interesting. Yes, I will think about it. Thank you for letting me know."

Adrenalin was pumping and my heart was racing. *Why*, I wondered, *does this excite me so much?*

As Alice talked, a tug of war was taking place within me. The practical me knew that we had no extra money for a college class. Andrew's expenses were making it difficult to meet our bills each month. Villanova was an hour's drive, and I would have to leave the children with Lawrence for half the weekend. On the other hand, the teacher in me had an incredibly strong desire to learn what it was that was making a difference for Andrew.

As if she could read my thoughts, Alice said, "We only meet four more times, and although it may be hard for you to give up those weekends, I know you will be glad you made the effort. Think what it will mean to Andrew for you to understand how he is learning."

"Could you hold on for a minute?" I asked Alice. Lawrence was looking at me quizzically. "It's Alice Koontz on the phone. She is teaching an Orton-Gillingham class at Villanova and she thinks I should take it. What do you think?"

He shrugged, a gesture that I had come to recognize as, "I'm not crazy about the idea, but I won't oppose you if you choose to do it."

That was all I needed. "Alice, I'll be there!" I said with genuine excitement. "Where do you meet?"

She gave me directions and I hung up the phone, filled with a sense of expectancy that I didn't fully understand.

From the first night, I loved the class! My mind was alive. Every fiber in my being strained to take in all that Alice was telling us about our language. It was all so new to me. How could I have been a functioning, literate adult for so long and not known how regular and even scientific our language is? Each spelling rule, each syllable division formula, each tip for integrating the muscles with the eyes and the ears, excited me. Between classes, I hungrily read the material that Alice had assigned us. Since I am generally a very level, unexcitable person, my reaction to all of this was puzzling. Was this a passing interest, or had this come into my life for a purpose? Only time would tell.

The last class came too soon. Alice stopped me on the way out the door for our lunch break. "The next class will be held at Johns Hopkins next semester. I want you in it."

"Johns Hopkins," I gulped. "I thought that this course was all there was."

"Oh, no," Alice explained. "There are two more in Baltimore. Next semester and summer school."

"Exactly when will this next class be taught?" I asked, fighting a hoard of negative thoughts.

"It's a night class," Alice answered. "Seven-thirty until ten. Starts in February." Looking at my expression, she added, "If you don't feel like driving afterwards, you can always spend the night at my house."

As I returned home that night, the practical me thought of many very good reasons for not taking the class. *Lawrence will be uncomfortable with the idea of my driving to Baltimore and returning late at night. If I stay overnight at Alice's house, who will get the children off to school?* This had always been my job and I wasn't sure my undomesticated husband would even know how to make a breakfast. Yet, I was hungry to learn more. What should I do?

Years later with Alice

The Trip

Our first opportunity to visit Andrew came in late October. Lawrence and I made plans to spend the day and observe the school. The train trips to and from Baltimore had become routine by now. Kara's jealousy had been tamed, and although I never left the station on Sunday night without a lump in my throat, I got over my sadness quickly. How could I be sad when he was learning and his self-confidence was growing? The Simonettis were people who were enriching his life with experiences he wouldn't have had at home. If he had to live apart from us, he was in the best possible situation.

The day was glorious! Brilliant golds and reds lined the highway on the way to Jemicy. My spirit matched the vibrant scenery. We enjoyed riding in silence, happy in our own thoughts.

It had been two months since Andrew left home. We had decided to send him to Jemicy with no assurance that this would end his struggle to read; but from what we could observe, he was making progress. I felt optimistic and couldn't wait to hear first hand what strides he had made.

This time as we entered the school, the enormous dog sprawled on the steps was a welcoming sight. I petted his head as I stepped over him. He opened one eye and I heard the "thump, thump, thump" of his tail as we walked down the hall.

"David's out of his office for a few minutes, but just make yourself at home," Barbara cheerfully greeted us. David's office was warm and comfortable, something I hadn't noticed on our first visit. Posters adorned the walls with encouraging, "can-do" captions. The furniture was soft and colorful. His desk was piled high with papers. I could tell that much of the pile was done in childish script. How good it was that this administrator was so involved with his students.

Abruptly, the door flew open and in walked a very tall clown. "Oh, excuse me. David's not here?"

Startled, Lawrence responded, "No. We're waiting for him. I'm Larry Biasotto and this is my wife, Ginger."

"Glad to meet you," the clown extended his hand. "I'm Joe Chitchester. Andrew's a good boy. Sure can talk. You here for a conference?"

"Yes, we drove down from Wilmington this morning. We're really looking forward to seeing all of his teachers and hearing first hand how he is doing," I beamed at Joe. "He has talked so much about you and your class. Science is definitely his favorite subject." Pausing, I looked him up and down. "What's with the clown costume?"

Joe looked as if it were the first time that he realized how he was dressed. "Oh, I always dress up for Halloween," he laughed. "All the faculty does. The kids like it." He turned to leave. "Stop by my room last period. That's when Andrew will be in class. Nice to meet you." He was gone.

"Nice guy," Lawrence commented. "I can see why Andrew likes him."

We waited a few minutes longer before David walked in, followed by a white ball of fur named Fiver. "Sorry to keep you waiting," David said, shaking our hands. Fiver growled. "One of our teachers is out today, and I had to get her class started. You know, sometimes I think that if none of the faculty showed up, the school would run without them."

I smiled, remembering when he had first told us that, but leaving a class to run by itself certainly proved his point.

"There's a great deal of structure here," David continued. "The kids know exactly where they are to be every minute of the day. There are also definite things that they do every day at the same time so these routines are firmly established. We are relaxed in many ways, but they know their limits."

I liked the picture he was painting. Children do need structure, and for children with learning differences, it is crucial.

"I guess you want to see Andrew. He should be in math about now." David wrote down Andrew's schedule. Fiver barked menacingly as we rose to leave. "Hush, dog," David scolded, scooping up the wriggling ball of fluff. "This is not a very friendly dog," he apologized, "but so far he hasn't bitten anyone." We assured him that we understood, and hurried off to find the math class.

The fall air was nippy as we walked the short distance from the main school to the outbuilding where math was taught. As we approached, I wondered what this space had been used for when the property was a dairy farm instead of a school. The room was long and narrow. The boys, nine of them, sat in a long line of tables facing the blackboard while a boyish looking teacher helped one of the students with a problem. No one paid much attention to us as we stood watching Andrew complete his day's assignment. He gave us a grin when we came in, but other than that, he made no attempt to leave his seat. *That's a change,* I thought. Before, any excuse to avoid work was readily taken.

When the class ended, the teacher walked over and introduced himself. "You must be Andrew's parents. I'm Mark Westerfelt. I heard you were coming today. He is doing fine. Nice boy."

We would have liked to have chatted longer, but Andrew was heading toward the main building at a clip. We cut our conversation with Mark short and hurried after him.

"What's the big rush?" Lawrence asked Andrew, as we walked inside.

"Tutoring with Nancy," he said, heading for the stairs.

This is what I had been waiting for. At last I would get to see the Orton-Gillingham approach being used with our son. Lawrence chose to relax in the faculty lounge, and Andrew and I climbed the narrow steps that led to the tutoring rooms.

Nancy smiled warmly as we came in. "Do you mind if I watch? I'm really interested in seeing you teach," I asked.

"Be glad to have you join us. Have a seat in our only spare chair."

The next hour was an absolute delight to me. I watched Andrew proceed through a structured phonetic program with rapt attention and obvious pleasure at his accomplishments. The fear of failure was gone in this success-oriented environment. He was learning to unravel the mystery of language, and he was feeling good about it. *How amazing it is,* I thought, *that after seven years of school failure, he still has the resilience to try.*

I sent a *thank you* heavenward for Nancy and her patient, quiet spirit. What an incredible gift she was to us!

We had been warned to bring a lunch since there was no cafeteria at Jemicy. Andrew found a space for us to join him in his homeroom. It seemed strange to me that his lunch was packed by someone else. I looked curiously inside. "Well, Andrew. I see that there is no junk food in this bag!"

"Not allowed," he said with a mouthful of peanut butter. "David is very strict about what we eat." Then he rattled off a list of "no-no's."

"I think it's great that they care about your bodies as well as your minds," I said enthusiastically.

Andrew shrugged. "I miss Tasty Cakes and potato chips."

I didn't look at Lawrence for fear that I would see him nodding in agreement.

A bell rang, and automatically the boys and girls cleaned up their lunch papers and began to leave the room. "What happens now?" Lawrence asked.

"It's quiet reading time," Andrew answered. "We each can go anywhere in the school for twenty minutes to read our book."

It had warmed up outside and I saw many children stretched out on the grass in the sun reading. *What an amazing, wonderful sight*, I thought. *All those dyslexic children reading!*

There was a picnic table right outside Andrew's classroom and the three of us went out there. "How about reading out loud to us so I can tell if I'm getting my money's worth," Lawrence joked with his son.

"Sure, Dad," Andrew replied, and began.

The words came haltingly, sound by sound, as he moved across the page, but that was progress. Before, reading had been a guessing game, and each sentence was a hodge-podge of misread words.

"Andrew," his father said as he reached the end of the page. "That was terrific! Keep going."

He turned the page and steadily decoded the symbols, missing only a few. When the bell rang for recess, only three pages had been read.

"Hey, it's a beginning," Lawrence said, sensing my thoughts. We watched Andrew run off with his friends. Neither of us spoke for a few minutes. "OK, what's next?" Lawrence said, getting to his feet.

Jemicy School required that each child participate in an after-school sport. After taxing their minds for six hours, they seemed glad to let off steam. The children took pride in being a part of Jemicy's teams. Even though there were fewer than 100 students, the school had a reputation for toughness and was a top competitor among the private schools of Baltimore. This was soccer season and we were going to see our son in his role of team goalie.

We sat on the grass and watched the practice. Their coach was the math teacher whom we had met earlier in the day. Mark insisted that the boys take their positions seriously. They were allowed little fooling around on the field. They were children, but the high standards being set for them academically carried onto the playing field. *How easy it would be*, I thought, *for the school to dismiss at 3 pm*. Jemicy's after-school sports program involved most of the regular staff. The teachers could certainly use the time to relax and get ready for the next day, but I noticed that no one left until after soccer practice was over. *They must do most of their preparation at night*, I thought, impressed by their dedication.

Unbelievable

Lawrence and I worked hard getting ready for our Due Process hearing. The endless reports and testimonials were stacked on my desk and sometimes I felt as if the typewriter was an extension of my arms. We tried to anticipate any argument the school district might present and took turns being the devil's advocate.

One morning, two weeks before the hearing, the phone rang. I put down the dish I was washing, dried my hands and picked up the phone. The voice on the other end identified herself as a representative of the New Castle County School District. Her voice was warm and friendly. "Mrs. Biasotto," she said, "yesterday a committee met to discuss possible placement for your son, Andrew, within the structure of our school district." She paused. "Mrs. Biasotto, we agreed unanimously to recommend funding for outside placement since we have nothing to offer him. I will send you forms to fill out and you will be reimbursed for all expenses incurred during this school year. This will include room, board and transportation."

I tried to comprehend her words. She was telling me that private placement was *their choice* for Andrew. We didn't have to face a hearing officer and try to defend our position. The district had agreed unanimously that they couldn't teach Andrew to read! It was over, and we had won without a hearing!

I could hardly believe it. So many people had prepared us to lose. We believed without doubt that Andrew was a perfect example of the complex child who had fallen through the cracks of the educational system, but it was almost unheard of for the school to admit to not being able to provide an adequate education. The word "adequate" had been the stumbling block to so many parents. It was a term that could be interpreted in different ways. Webster defined it as "barely sufficient or satisfactory." I knew of many parents who had tried and failed to prove that their child's education was not satisfactory. This morning I was getting the news that the district agreed with us that Andrew's was not.

I thanked the lady from the District office with heart-felt gratitude. The warmth of her tone indicated to me that this was one phone call that she had been happy to make. When I hung up, I shrieked at the dog, "We won! We won! We don't have to go through a hearing. It's over. We won!" Dropping to my knees on the rug in front of the kitchen sink, I gave thanks. Jemicy, Nancy, and now this!

I got to my feet, walked to the phone and dialed my husband. "You'll never guess what just happened…"

Visionaries

I went to Johns Hopkins. A new friend from the Villanova class drove down with me. Some nights we accepted Alice's invitation to spend the night, but most of the time we drove back, getting home around midnight.

One of the requirements for this second course was a research paper and presentation to the class on a related topic. Having been newly introduced to brain differences, I chose the brain as my subject to research. In 1979, there was very little information about learning and the brain. I plowed through many books that described brain trauma and brain surgery, but there was little about education. Gradually, I compiled a brief history of brain research from the early 1800's until the present.

"Before 1800," I began the presentation, "most people believed that the two hemispheres of the brain were created for the same purpose, just as our eyes and ears are. It was assumed that one was a spare."

For the next hour, I described the brain research of Gall, Bouillard, Auburtin, Broca and Pfefer. As I warmed to my subject, my nervousness disappeared. The women in the class seemed to be genuinely interested.

"In the United States, Dr. Samuel T. Orton, a professor of neuro-psychiatry and neuro-pathology at Columbia University, came to the conclusion that reading disabilities were caused by a lack of cerebral dominance. He believed that letters and word symbols are recorded on both sides of the brain in mirrored patterns. As handedness develops, one hemisphere should take control. Some people are not decidedly right-handed and some are not decidedly left-handed. Orton felt that the more one hemisphere has control, the more able one is to use language. If a child does not develop a dominant hemisphere, then the image on the non-dominant side sometimes asserts itself in reverse patterns. Thus we have letter confusion, b-d, p-g, b-p, m-w, n-u and word reversals, was-saw, dog-god…"

"Much of Dr. Orton's findings came from his work with boys in the New York schools who were obviously smart but doing poorly in school. He worked with a school psychologist, Anna Gillingham, to create a plan of instruction that was successful in reversing the tide of failure in these boys. This systematic instruction became known as the Orton-Gillingham approach to reading, writing and spelling. It has worked for many children and it is now working with my son, Andrew. It is the reason for my return to the field of education."

I looked back at my notes. "Although Dr. Orton's theories have never been proven, Dr. Archie Silver, in a neurological evaluation of children in 1949, proved that nine out of ten children whose reading level is below their mental age have problems which may be related to the establishment of a dominant cerebral hemisphere. Ninety-two per cent of these children had defects in right-left orientation."

"Likewise, in Paul Schilder's 'extension of arms' test, learning disabled children showed evidence of mixed dominance. When asked to close their eyes, extend their arms parallel to the floor, and spread their fingers, one arm tended to be higher than the other. It was assumed that the arm with the greater muscle tone would be higher, thus indicating the dominant hemisphere. With learning disabled children, 74% showed a discrepancy in the higher hand and the writing hand. (Right-handed children raised their left arms higher.) Another 18% showed no elevation. He administered the test again to 100 third and fourth graders. Thirty-four of the forty-one who were reading below their mental age showed a discrepancy in the raised hand and the writing one. Of the remaining seven, four didn't fit in the L.D. category. Three couldn't be accounted for."

"Here we are in 1979," I began my conclusion, "and we still don't know precisely what causes one child to read easily, while another with similar intelligence, fails to read."

A woman in the front of the class raised her hand. "You mentioned earlier that until recently there was little research concerning the two hemispheres of the brain. Surely with new information coming out, we can understand more about why some children don't read from studying the left and right hemispheres. Can you shed some light on this subject?"

"Yes. We are beginning to understand the function of the hemispheres. Research coming from autopsies of stroke and war victims has placed language in the left temporal lobe. Experiments on those afflicted with seizures have helped garner information about the functions of the hemispheres. Doctors have severed the corpus callosum in patients whose seizures were so severe that they couldn't function, and then tested them by anesthetizing each side of the brain and performing tests. What they have discovered is that the left side governs the right side of the body. It is verbal, analytical, symbolic, abstract, temporal, and rational. The right hemisphere controls the left side of the body. In contrast, it is nonverbal, concerned with the present moment, and sees likenesses and relationships. The right brain is also non-temporal, non-rational, spatial (sees how parts relate to wholes), intuitive and holistic (perceives overall patterns and structures). It's the right hemisphere that recognizes a familiar face in a crowded airport, sees how a room should be arranged, or sees how to fix a piece of machinery. The left hemisphere, on the other-hand plays a vital part in school success."

"Can you explain the function of the left and right hemisphere in the area of reading?" Alice Koontz spoke up.

"Because of the complexity of the brain, both hemispheres are involved in the reading process," I began. "The left side analyzes phonological and lexical properties of words."

I saw a few puzzled expressions and clarified. "*Phonological* means the study of speech sounds. The study of speech sounds in a language is a science. The left brain picks up these sounds and remembers them. *Lexical* means relating to the vocabulary of a language. Words presented to the left hemisphere are named more easily than if presented to the right. We know that the left hemisphere is the location for the language center in most English speaking people. Another interesting fact about the brain concerns its adaptability. If for some reason the left hemisphere is destroyed prior to the age of seven or eight, the language center will shift to the right hemisphere."

"If the left side houses the language center, then what part does the right play in reading?" asked one of the students.

"The right hemisphere's spatial function is important in beginning reading when children are learning to recognize letters and words as gestalts (shapes, forms, configurations). Both receive and process information separately, but work together in establishing patterns. There is a danger in thinking that recognition of word shapes is teaching reading. It is only a small part. Children need to know the code and how to create words by blending sounds represented by alphabetic symbols. They also need to understand the concept of syllables and how long words can be broken down into small pieces."

"When we are teaching multisensory, structured language, we are actually creating connections in the brain. For some reason, good readers know automatically how to divide words into syllables. They know what the letters sound like. They remember spelling rules through seeing the correct spelling of words while reading. Dyslexic children don't do this automatically, but when taught the relationship of sound to symbol, syllable division rules and spelling expectancies, they can read almost as well as the non-disabled readers. We have to help them to put into their brains what they need to know in order to decode and encode words. We know it works. I know it works because it is working for my son."

Several members of the class clapped their support. I wondered if they, too, had children who struggled to read.

"I would like to conclude this presentation about the brain with some facts and an opinion. The brain weighs 1.5 kilograms. It is the most complex apparatus in the universe. It is basically unchanging. Its normal state is to be aggressive. Only in sleep is it passive. It needs to make sense of the world and exact meaningful patterns from confusion. The brain is the computer of the mind, and only as we study its workings can we begin to grasp what it means to be human. Although scientists may see dyslexia as a failure of the brain to perform, I feel that even more, it is a failure on the part of us who are educators to teach. There are children out there with creative, wonderful minds who are falling through the cracks because our schools don't know how to teach them. We in this room have learned that there is a way that works, and I believe that it is our moral duty to do what we can to share it with others."

My face was flushed and my heart was pounding in my chest when I sat down. Somehow I knew that my words were directed at me.

Wisdom

The highlight of the year at Jemicy came in April when the Science Fair was held. Dyslexic children often excel in science because of strong spatial abilities in the right hemisphere of their brains.

The Fruit Dehydrator

Our experience with science fairs had been along the lines of a parent/child endeavor. Usually the parent did the most work. At Jemicy, the children were not allowed to do the work at home. Each child, under the supervision of Joe Chitchester, made his/her own creation. The final exhibit was nothing short of spectacular. In the gymnasium an elevator based on the pulley system went up and down from floor to ceiling. Plastic lined a low area outside and it was filled with water. In it an actual submarine with a child inside submerged and rose at the whim of the crowd. One boy's exhibit had a blue ribbon on it. I learned that it had won first place at the Johns Hopkins Science Fair. All of the exhibits had been made from scrap materials, and Andrew had built a fruit dehydrator. I decided that he must be planning to feed dried fruit to the whole school because it was seven feet long and three feet wide. David generously offered to let us take it home for our own use, but eying its size, Lawrence prudently declined.

It was a great night. The boys who had failed in other schools were finally the focus of admiration by adults and peers alike. For several days, groups of children from other schools made their way through the gymnasium admiring the creative genius they saw. The event was not without humor, however. Needing to use the bathroom, one of the boys left a sign on his exhibit:

COLSED DU NOT TUCH

In the beginning of May, we met with David for our final conference. Andrew had made excellent progress, but because he was so far behind, David recommended that he go to Dunnabeck, a seven week tutoring camp near Pittsburgh. We knew that David was right, but we wanted Andrew to enjoy a relaxed summer with his family. Our faces must have reflected our feelings because two days later I received a letter from Ginny Logan, the new secretary.

Dear Ginger,

Your son Andrew is a delightful person and I love him dearly. He's had a lot of homework lately and has opted not to visit us yet. I'm sure when he's ready he'll come. It's entirely up to him.

You brought back memories when you came out of your parent conference. I could see the sadness in your eyes. Remember. This too shall pass.

We're lucky at Jemicy to have such committed teachers. It's wonderful to know that many of the staff are praying as well as working with the children! I often wonder if there will ever be an end to this anguish and I have to recall the words of St. Paul: "Now hope that is seen is not hope. For who hopes for what he sees? But if we hope for what we do not see, we wait for it with patience." Romans 8:24

Pat Covington reminded me of Philippians 2:8, which stresses that we should focus on the positive elements and not the negative. "Whatever is pure, lovely, gracious, if there is any excellence, if there is anything worthy of praise, THINK ABOUT THESE THINGS!"

If we could just remember that, we'd be a lot better off. Be of good cheer. Hang in there and know that you are not alone.

With much love, shalom,
    A fellow mother,
    Ginny Logan

Ginny's letter was like water in the desert. I needed her encouragement. Being a parent of a special needs child can be a lonely business, and it is good to know that others are standing with you.

Over his loud protestations, Andrew went to Dunnabeck. This time an airplane took him away, and because he didn't want to go, it was particularly hard on all of us.

Since we were allowed only one visit in the middle of the summer, many letters went back and forth. Andrew was required to write them and family members responded.

Dear Fanily,

It's Friday the 6th I wint uater sking and caut a lot of liseds I cept to for pets I'n lerning how to tipe I lernd the alfabit in 2 days I hope to tipe a leter son I'll tech kara if sele let me.

I ges kara's leter got lost in the male or at camp.

I an rely disaponted. I can't wate to get home. I rely miss yoy

love,

Andrw

Dear Andrew,

I heard about my letter not getting to you. I'm very sorry about that, because I was looking forward to a return letter from you.

As you may know, I am visiting Grammy and Grampy for 10 days. Mom called last night to read me your last 2 letters. You caught two lizards. Yuck. Did they fight? Why did you let them go?

So hows the camp? What kinds of things do you do, beside catching lizards?

So how much smarter are you now? Knowing you, you're probably in college grades. You're so smart! If I said, "Andrew what happened in 1771?" You'd know.

I miss you so much but I have to go know because my hand is killing me!

Love,

Kara

P.S. This letter better get there!! Write back.

Diana Hanbury King, the camp director and head of the Kildonan School, impressed us greatly when we met her at Parent's Weekend. Her quiet, confident demeanor was the result of many years of involvement with dyslexic children.

Listening to Diana King speak about the gifts of these children who struggle to read and spell made me think that perhaps they were the lucky ones. Their gifts of creativity, spatial understanding and holistic thinking were beyond my grasp. She told us about one young man who, when asked if he would trade his gifts for the ability to read and write easily, said, "No." His gifts were special and he knew it.

I don't think that Diana was purposely giving us a pep talk, but she lit a fire in me to share the truth. Dyslexia isn't a genetic mistake. It is a gift!

AudacitY

At summer camp in 1979, while Andrew was polishing his reading skills with Diana King, I was taking two courses at Johns Hopkins. Finally I had come to the point of being able to leave home without feeling guilty. Larry was sixteen and Kara was twelve. With the help of grandparents, they were doing a good job of looking after each other. I loved walking around the campus of Johns Hopkins University with the young undergraduates. Being there made me realize what I didn't understand when I was a college student. Education is a privilege.

Alice Koontz was a good teacher. Her knowledge of the English language was endless. Every time she explained a new rule, I would marvel all over again at the regularity of our language. Everything was so exciting.

After completing summer school, I would be ready to teach. The approach stimulated me, and I couldn't wait to share it with children like Andrew. There would be, I felt sure, no problem getting a job. A private school had offered me a position tutoring, and if I didn't get a job in a public school, I would take that. Life was good. My enthusiasm knew no bounds.

It came, therefore, as a shock to learn that my specialized training didn't automatically impress people. I called and sent out résumés, but no school was interested. "What is Orton-Gillingham?" a few asked. When I explained multisensory, structured language as briefly as I could, they would say, "Hmm, sounds interesting," or something to that effect. Then they would hang up after telling me that my name was on file and if something came along, they would give me a call.

It appeared that I would need to accept the tutoring job at the private school, but when I called to ask for more information, I received a shock. "I'm sorry, Mrs. Biasotto, but the position of tutor has been filled."

"But I was offered the job in June after my interview," I explained to the secretary. "They told me they would hold it for me until August."

"I'm truly sorry, but I don't even have a record of your application."

There I was. All dressed up and no place to go. Everything in me burned with the desire to teach children like Andrew. *Without Jemicy, who knows what his life would be like. Now he has a chance. There are many who will never have a chance. Their lives will be crippled because they can't read.* I remembered the blond boy in the Intensive Learning Center. These thoughts were like gasoline on a fire. I burned to do something for children and their parents who had no Jemicy.

If they won't hire me, as least they are going to learn what they are missing! I said to myself as I compiled a list of schools to visit. A year ago, I would never have had the courage or audacity to knock on a principal's door and try to instruct her in the needs of some of her students. Now, filled with purpose, I made the calls. Some invited me to come to their offices to talk.

Others were polite, but unreceptive. No one opened the door any farther. It was very discouraging.

One of my last calls was to Dr. Sandra Worthen, who was Delaware Governor DuPont's education advisor. She invited me to come to her office in downtown Wilmington. As I spoke, she listened attentively to my explanation of the reading needs of some children whose brains didn't respond to the *look-say* method. I could see in her face that she was with me, but my heart fell when, at the end of my visit, she said, "I am not in a position to do anything, but have you talked to Dr. Ann Houseman? She is the reading specialist for the state."

So many times I had heard the words, "I can't help you, but…" This sounded like another dead end.

"No. I haven't talked to Dr. Houseman," I answered her.

She reached for her phone. "Let me call her office and make an appointment for you to meet with her right here in my office." She dialed and quickly arranged with Dr. Houseman's secretary for us to meet the following week.

I felt jubilant as I left her office. *This may be the person who can make things happen,* I thought hopefully.

A week later, loaded with books and materials bearing evidence of the reading approach that I was trying to promote, I headed for Dr. Worthen's office. Traffic was heavy as I made my way downtown. Parking was usually a problem, but as I approached the State Building, I spotted a car pulling out just ahead. *A good omen,* I thought.

Waiting outside Dr. Worthen's office, I thumbed through the pile of papers in my lap. Project Read in Minnesota had been using their version of Dr. Orton's program for ten years with a 1.2 year gain for children in their lowest reading groups. Many students never needed the services of the Special Education teachers because, through this program, they were able to keep up with their peers.

Allett Cox had trained therapists to teach small groups of children in Dallas, Texas. The results were impressive, and now their efforts were spreading.

Winston Salem, North Carolina had kept records on children taught by the Orton-Gillingham method and compared their progress to a control group that had been taught by a whole-word reading program. After three years, the Orton group surpassed the control group by a third.

After a few minutes, Dr. Worthen came out and invited me into her office. Dr. Houseman hadn't arrived yet, so we chatted about local events. I looked at my watch. "Dr. Houseman is quite late," Dr. Worthen concurred. "Perhaps I should call her office."

I knew this was too easy, I thought as Dr. Worthen spoke to someone on the other end of the line.

She motioned me to take the take the phone. "Dr. Houseman's secretary put the appointment on the wrong day," she whispered.

"Hello, Dr. Houseman," I began. "Dr. Worthen…"

"So sorry about the mix-up," Dr. Houseman cut in. "I hear you would like to see Orton-Gillingham taught in public schools."

"Yes," I replied, but before I could begin my sales pitch, she spoke again. Her words nearly left me speechless.

"I know about the Orton approach. How can I help you?"

"I guess the first step would be to educate the teachers," I answered, haltingly. I hadn't expected to be asked to recommend a path forward and my mind raced ahead, thinking of the successful programs I had been prepared to tell her about. "Perhaps an in-service for teachers could be arranged."

"Would you be able to teach it?" Dr. Houseman asked directly. She certainly didn't waste any words.

"Oh, no!" I said emphatically, "but I'm sure Alice Koontz, my teacher from Johns Hopkins, would be able to do it. When do you think a class could be held?"

"It's too late for the fall catalogue, but if you get her to agree, then we can schedule it for the spring."

"I'll get right on it," I said with conviction. "This is just great. I don't know how to thank you."

"No need," she answered brusquely. "Call me when you have set a date with Alice Koontz. Then I will arrange the location."

Elated, I hung up the phone. Dr. Worthen grinned at me. "Success?" she asked with a knowing smile.

"Success," I answered, giving her two thumbs up. If her desk hadn't been between us she would also have gotten a hug.

Zeal

It came to our attention that a child who had been identified as "rare or complex" was eligible for twelve-month placement. Even though Andrew had not been in the same school for twelve months, he did qualify under the law. Once again we applied for a Due Process hearing. This time there was no eleventh hour reprieve.

Our hearing officer was from Temple University. He was all business and conducted the hearing like a trial. We were prepared with arguments, signed opinions from those who had either examined Andrew or taught him, and test evidence that indicated why he needed summer help.

After four hours, those representing the school district concluded their arguments. The law required that Andrew be given an adequate education, not the best possible education. They felt, therefore, that summer school was not necessary.

Two weeks later, a thick envelope from Temple University arrived in the mail. I opened it apprehensively. Choosing not to read the long discourse, I skimmed to the back page. There was no clear decision that I could see, so I started over again, reading every word. This time there was one sentence that I clearly understood. "Due to the fact that in May, Andrew Biasotto was still three years below grade level in reading, summer school is a necessary part of his education plan."

We were elated. This was a big victory because never before had twelve-month funding been awarded to a child whose handicap was reading.

As expected, the District appealed. One month later, we received word from a second hearing officer that she concurred with the first decision. Our expenses for the summer school would be forthcoming.

Dr. Houseman's voice was crisp and businesslike. "I'm afraid I have some bad news about your Orton-Gillingham in-service. Yesterday, I learned that I would be changing jobs. I begin next week as principal of Martin Luther King Elementary School in Wilmington. Since I will no longer be Reading Supervisor for the State, I will not be able to arrange training classes for teachers." She paused, waiting for my reaction. When I didn't say anything, she continued. "If you don't get a job, would you consider training parents to teach non-readers at my school?"

I was having trouble focusing on all that she had said. My thoughts zeroed in on the fact that there would be no teacher training. Somehow this seemed like the biggest blow of all. Orton-Gillingham had come so close to being put into the hands of teachers, but now that door was closed.

There was silence on her end of the phone. "Dr. Houseman," I said slowly. "I am terribly disappointed that the in-service has been cancelled. Teaching teachers is the best way to reach the children. I appreciate your asking me to train parents, but I don't feel qualified to do that. I could teach a child to read, but to teach others to teach children…I don't know."

"If you should change your mind, give me a call. I like your zeal and there are a lot of non-readers at Martin Luther King who could use Orton-Gillingham training," she concluded.

After we hung up, I sat for a long time staring into space. I remembered how I had felt as I read through the Gillingham/Stillman textbook, *Remedial Training*. Each day, as I opened it to read another chapter, I wondered if the adrenalin would stop and the exhilaration would go away. It didn't and it hasn't.

I remembered the glowing faces of the students at Jemicy and the face of the little boy in the Intensive Learning Center who seemed to ask, "And what will you do for me?"

I remembered the last year and a half of study under Alice Koontz, the utter joy of learning new and important things. Was it to be just for my own edification, or would I be able to use it to help children who struggle to read?

The fire burned.

When it seemed clear that there would be no teaching job, I forced myself to think seriously about Dr. Houseman's proposal. I knew that in order for volunteers to teach students, they would need an instruction manual with a step-by-step progression. There was none. Could I possibly organize this vast amount of material in such a way that parents with no training in reading could learn it in a short period of time? The challenge was daunting, and yet…there was nothing else. *What do I have to lose?* I asked myself. *Time? I have plenty of that.*

Pride? No one likes to fail, but I could handle that. OK, Dr. Houseman. I will take your challenge. You give me the tutors, and I will put together a program. I picked up the phone and dialed.

Epilogue

Dr. Houseman recruited five volunteers that fall in 1979. They taught five sixth grade boys with a simple 26-page manual. After only four months of tutoring, the boys began to make substantial gains. Their teachers noted improvements in behavior, as well in their academic subjects, including math. One boy who was tested by the school psychologist advanced four grade levels in reading! The next year, thanks to his tutor who followed him into junior high school, he was able to leave special education classes and return to the mainstream. Four of the volunteers continued tutoring children into the 90s.

As a result of the success of these first volunteers, a few educational diagnosticians recommended Orton-Gillingham on IEP's. This caused significant consternation in administrative circles because there were no Orton-Gillingham trained teachers and IEP requirements excluded volunteers. I was hopeful that a teacher training class might be offered, but it wasn't until years later.

My comfort level with multisensory, structured language increased as I taught dyslexic students in two small private schools the following year. It was sheer joy to watch them make sense out of the mysterious squiggles on the page.

In June of 1982, Jonquil Kail, a tutor who was dyslexic herself, arranged for me spend three weeks at the Dyslexia Institute in London, England observing how Orton-Gillingham was used in small group instruction. Those at the Institute were surprised to learn that although Dr. Samuel Orton was from the United States, his work was not used throughout our schools. Many ideas for group instruction, plus a pattern for wooden letters and dozens of games, came back across the Atlantic with me.

Later that same year, the White Clay Kiwanis Club in Newark, Delaware invited me to speak to their club about dyslexia. At the end of the evening, they made an offer. "You create a program to help these kids, and we will pay for it!" This was totally unexpected and a bit overwhelming. For the next few weeks, two models competed in my brain. One was the volunteer model that was working well in several public schools, and the other was the small group model that had been used in London. After much thought, I chose the volunteer model. More children could be reached with volunteers, and it was a lot cheaper.

Members of the Kiwanis and I met with the State Superintendent of Schools and the Director of Special Services before launching a full scale drive to recruit volunteers. We explained that it would be the school's job to help select the most appropriate students, get permission from their parents for tutoring, and give us a private place to work. The Kiwanis would take care of all expenses. Our program was heartily supported. We thought we were in.

Word of this reading project spread quickly in the community, and twenty volunteers signed up for training. Three schools were requested in the northern part of the New Castle County School District, and one school in the southern part, to accommodate where the tutors were living.

After explaining to administrative personnel that we had the approval of the State Superintendent, I expected to be welcomed with open arms. Not so. After several months and many phone calls, they tentatively agreed to give us one school. I tried to explain that fifteen volunteers would be too many for one school. There wouldn't be space for all of them to work.

Weeks passed. When we spoke again, I was told that they had discussed it and decided not to give us any schools. I was stunned and incredulously asked, "Why?" The reply left me speechless. "Because that would be showing favoritism to your method."

Luckily, the superintendent from the southern part of the district had a different attitude. "Sure, we would love to have your tutors," he said. "We can use all the help we can get." Three months later, eighteen very motivated volunteers completed their training and Project ASSIST (Alphabetic Sound Symbol Instruction Systematically Taught) was officially launched.

Each year thereafter, a fall class for volunteers has been held. The professionalism of these individuals and the success they have with their students has motivated teachers to learn more about this approach to reading. The first class for teachers took place in 1986 around my dining room table. Many of those who came did so because they had witnessed their non-reading students begin to learn with instruction from a volunteer.

During the mid-eighties two major events influenced the evolution of Project ASSIST. One was Romalda Spalding's work, *The Writing Road to Reading.* I was exposed to this approach in a class taught by Marguerite Hoerl at the University of Delaware. It was there that I learned the value of spelling by sounds rather than by letter names. As Marguerite instructed, my brain churned with ideas. The result was a complete revision and expansion of the manual.

The second event was an open door into the DuPont Company's Educational Research Department. Through books, videos and classes, I gleaned a great deal about how people learn. By integrating art, music and drama (right hemisphere) with reading, writing and spelling (left hemisphere), strong memory is established. This needs to be done in a teaching environment where the student feels safe, and is relaxed. Also, children remember best by stories. Armed with this new found knowledge, I set out to revise the manual once again with the addition of music and art. Stories were created to teach important rules of the English language. The alphabet became people. The vowels were the girls and the consonants were their brothers. They interacted as families do. These *Fables by Phonograms* became an important teaching tool in the Project ASSIST curriculum.

In 1989, my husband helped me to incorporate into a non-profit 501(c)(3) charitable organization. "What would you like to be called?" he asked. "A corporation? A company?"

"I want to be an institute," I replied. "Project ASSIST Institute!" To his credit he didn't roll his eyes or even raise an eyebrow.

The tax rules specified that we needed to have a board of directors. Since I didn't want to show favoritism among the volunteers, I offered a seat on the board to any tutor who wanted to serve. Five signed up. Lisa Simon agreed to be our director, Betty Kane, our treasurer, Sue Muzzi, our secretary. Tona Huiner, Estelle Sawyer and I were members at large. Our annual budget was under $7,000.00.

Lisa Simon worked 20-25 hours a week as our volunteer director until it became clear that she needed to get a job to help pay tuitions for her sons. She announced her resignation at one of our monthly board meetings. "You can't quit! We need you!" we all said. "We'll find a way to pay you." And we did.

In the spring of 1992, a grant proposal was written to MBNA for $60,000. Not only was it accepted, but the bank's president, Mr. Charles Cawley, agreed to give us $30,000 for the next five years if we could raise an additional $30,000. We were jubilant! Now we could hire Lisa, rent office space at the Edgemoor Community Center, and get out of our kitchens!

Over the next few years, the organization grew. The curriculum evolved to include a pre-reading component, auditory discrimination through the awareness of how sounds are made in the mouth. The manual was refined to be usable by teachers as well as volunteers. A variety of language classes were held at our office site and in school districts throughout the state. New staff was hired. Our Board grew to represent the broader community, and the State of Delaware became a major contributor to our budget.

In 1999, we changed our name from Project ASSIST Institute to Reading ASSIST® Institute, to more clearly define what we do. We were no longer just a project. That same year, we sought and were approved for accreditation by the International Multisensory Structured Language Education Council (IMSLEC), and established a web site (www.readingassist.org).

All of this growth led to a need for more space, and in 2000 we moved to the Community Services Building in downtown Wilmington, Delaware. This building houses many of the nonprofits that serve the Delaware area.

After sixteen years as director of Reading ASSIST®, Lisa Simon retired in 2002. She left big shoes to fill. Culminating an extensive search, Rebecca Combs, a highly qualified professional from Rochester, NY, was chosen to replace her. Rebecca has proven to have big shoes, too. Under her leadership, Reading ASSIST® is training thousands of teachers and tutors in the Tri-State area who in turn are helping ever more children obtain the skill of reading and writing.

Initially Reading ASSIST®'s methods didn't have scientific support. Our observations were not enough to convince those in the literacy environment that structured, multisensory language instruction was necessary for the success of some of their students. But today research abounds that reinforces what we have observed for years. Brain imaging science has also validated our methods. Believers are everywhere.

We have a dream that no child will experience failure when success is possible. We know that highly trained teachers and engaged parents are essential for a child to become a fluent reader. We also know that it will require universities, schools, corporations, elected officials and concerned citizens to work together to ensure that teachers receive the depth of instruction that will enable them to meet the needs of all of their students. It can happen. It must happen. The journey won't be easy, but we have the map!

And as for Andrew

Celebrating with the Simonettis

When he graduated from Jemicy, he was thirteen and reading on an 8th grade level, a gain of six years. Nancy Simonetti, his beloved teacher/mother, was beside him as he received his diploma. Tragically, a month later, Nancy was struck down with a cancer that eventually took her life. "The two years Andrew stayed with us were the only two years of my life when that would have been possible," she told me shortly before her death. "God's timing was perfect." Words cannot describe the grief that overwhelmed me at her funeral. She had saved our child.

Andrew returned home to attend high school at Salesianum School, a boy's school in Wilmington, Delaware. Because of the creative paragraph he wrote on his entrance exam, Andrew was admitted, but under academic probation. Initially, his test grades went up and down like a yoyo. For several months, I experienced shallow breathing and no fingernails, but eventually he rose above the danger zone and we all began to relax.

The spring he graduated from Salesianum, Andrew met Kim Gerlach. Kim's mother, Jane, and I were friends. I played the matchmaker. Kim was also dyslexic, and I thought they had a lot in common and could be great friends. Little did I know how great. It may not have been love at first sight, but almost. Andrew worked at the Delaware shore the summer they met, and Kim often came to visit us at our beach house. The striking contrast of fair, redheaded Kim walking hand in hand with my tan, swarthy son remains a strong and happy memory.

That fall, Andrew began college at Salisbury State University. The school was very willing to accommodate him with books on tape, proofreaders and other supports. At first he took advantage of some of these things, but rather quickly discovered that if he went to every class and really listened, he didn't have to expend the energy to read the textbook. Once, when he needed some extra help, he sought out a smart girl and approached her by saying, "I hear the best way to learn something is by teaching someone else." She nodded in agreement. Then he gave her an opportunity she couldn't pass up. "How would you like to teach me?" Thus he arranged for private tutoring.

When he came home for Christmas after the first marking period, Andrew announced that he thought he was going to make the Dean's List. When he wasn't looking, Lawrence and I rolled our eyes. All his life he had been optimistic, but the chance that he could earn a 3.25 was not likely. The day the mail brought his grades, we watched him carefully as he opened the envelope. His expression didn't change as he looked at the paper. Finally, Lawrence said, "Well?"

Andrew didn't look up. He said quietly, "I was wrong."

Lawrence gave me a knowing look. "What did you get?" I asked, prepared to be sympathetic.

He looked up, grinning. "3.4!"

Kim and Andrew were married on August 12, 1988, the year they graduated from college. In a toast at his wedding, his brother, Larry lifted his glass and said, "Many of you know what a hard time Andrew had in school, but today, thanks to Kim, he is the happy one." It was true. The struggles of the past were behind him and a new chapter in his life had begun.

Jessica, their first child, was born two years later. I had never seen a more beautiful baby, but then I had never been a grandmother before.

Since dyslexia is usually inherited, we were watching Jessica for signs, and I was ready and eager to teach her everything I knew. She didn't disappoint us. Reading was a mystery for Jessica. *No problem,*

Happiness

I thought. *When she is ready, I will teach her how to read.* What I didn't take into consideration was that she didn't want her grandmother to be her teacher.

Jessica's dyslexia was almost as severe as her dad's. After two years in a school for children with learning differences, Jessica was still behind in reading and math. Kim and Andrew decided that their only option was to home-school her. Debbie DeGrosky, a skilled Reading ASSIST® instructor, taught her to read and write, and her grandfather, Howard Gerlach, taught her math. Today she is in high school and doing well.

Darby was born 2 ½ years after Jessica. She is not dyslexic but is a creative speller. Actually she is creative in all ways and is happiest when exercising her gifts of music and drama. One can't look into the future, but if Darby gets her wish, it will include Broadway.

Jacob, number three, seemed headed for reading problems. His speech was delayed and when he did begin to talk, he mispronounced many words. When he called Jane, his other grandmother, *Mig,* instead of *Gims* (Jessica's name for her), we raised collective eyebrows and prepared ourselves for another challenge. However, Kim taught Jacob all the sounds of the single letters before he went to school and prayed a lot. To our joy, he has never had any problems with reading and he excels academically. (In case he should ever read this book, I should add that he is also an excellent athlete.)

Tommy completes the family. At this writing, he is two, a bit young to exhibit signs of dyslexia, but if he does share this brain difference, we know what to do.

Jacob, Darby, Jessica and Tommy

Andrew's struggle to learn to read was definitely not what I would have chosen for him, but the experiences of his childhood helped to mold his character.

One of my proudest moments occurred at the Reading ASSIST® Student Appreciation Day when those children who completed the program received gold medals from their tutors. Jessica was one of the recipients and Andrew was "the successful dyslexic" who had been chosen to address the students and their parents. After giving a brief description of some of his trials, he said, "The Bible says we are fearfully and wonderfully made. Don't let the fact that you have had a hard time learning to read discourage you. You are exactly as God intended you to be. I'm sure you have talents that many who read and write easily don't have. I can fix almost anything. My hobby is fixing clocks. It's fun for me and I wouldn't trade my gifts for having had an easy time in school. You have worked hard and have finished Reading ASSIST®, so now you can read. Use this skill to help you develop your other talents and use those talents to help others."

Every child has a time to shine. For some, it is when they are young and in school. For Andrew, it was when he became a man.

Editor's Note:

On March 16, 2005, in Wilmington, Delaware, Virginia L. Biasotto received the Jefferson Award for extraordinary public service.

Delaware's Senator
Thomas Carper
formally presented
Virginia Biasotto with
the Jefferson Award at
a ceremony in
Washington, DC, on
June 21, 2005.

Printed in the United States
46603LVS00002B/157-204